WHAT
IS
BUDDHISM?

WHAT IS BUDDHISM?

AN ANSWER FROM THE WESTERN POINT OF VIEW

GYAN

Published by

Gyan Publishing House
5, Ansari Road
Daryaganj, New Delhi-110002
Phone: 011-47034999, 9811692060
E-mail: books@gyanbooks.com

Distribution Network
gyanbooks.com
India, USA, Canada, UK, Australia

ISBN: 978-93-7097-189-9 (PB)

First Published, 1928

2nd Impression 2025

Printed at: Gyan Press, Delhi.

WHAT IS BUDDHISM?

What is Buddhism?

An Answer from the Western Point of View.

COMPILED BY

THE BUDDHIST LODGE, LONDON.

1928.

Published by the BUDDHIST LODGE, LONDON,
at 121, St. George's Road, Westminster, S.W.1.

Dedication.

“ Truth is within ourselves; it takes no rise
From outward things, whate'er you may believe.
There is an inmost centre in us all,
Where truth abides in fulness; and around,
Wall upon wall, the gross flesh hems us in.
. . . . ‘ To *know* ’
Rather consists in opening out a way
Whence the imprisoned splendour may escape,
Than in effecting entry for a light
Supposed to be without.”

From Browning's Paracelsus.

This book is therefore

dedicated

to all who seek the Way to self-enlightenment.

Note.

Parts One, Two and Three of this book were originally published in serial form between February, 1927, and July, 1928, under the title, " A Reasoned Exposition of Buddhism from the Western point of view," in the Magazine "*Buddhism in England*," the organ of the Buddhist Lodge, London.

Preface.

"If anyone can convince me that some action of mine is wrong, I will cheerfully change: I seek the truth, which never yet hurt any man. What hurts is persisting in self-deceit and ignorance."

Marcus Aurelius.

The recent War proved many things, among them being the failure of Christianity to stand the acid test of emergency, and the danger of scientific knowledge ahead of national morality.

By the failure of orthodox Science and Religion, Westerners are forced to seek elsewhere for a solution to the problems facing them. Hence the increasing interest in "foreign" religions of every kind, among them Buddhism. The latter's all-pervading influence is due to its being at the same time scientific and religious, in the finest sense of the terms, for it is an aspect of the Wisdom which unites them both. But while Truth is one it may be presented in many forms, and in compiling a reply to the oft-repeated question—What is Buddhism?—we have prepared an answer from the Western point of view. Even as water may be poured into different coloured bottles, yet remain the same in each, so the Teaching of the All-Enlightened One may be presented in a dozen different ways according to the needs of those to whom it is given.

As Buddhism is part of Truth it is to be found in every land, and is the property in some degree of every poet, mystic and philosopher. Throughout the book, therefore, in quoting others' words as perfectly expressing what we wish to say, we have chosen those of Western writers in addition to the Buddhist Scriptures, to the end that we may show how the Dhamma is no alien philosophy but may be found, in fragmentary form, among the thinkers of the West.

In order that our readers may examine these quotations for themselves we append a Bibliography of books from which quotation has been made. As our aim is rather a popular manual than a scholarly treatise we have used the Pali or Sanscrit form of a word according as one or the other is better known in the West, and make no apologies for inconsistency.

The whole book is in fact a compromise. Compiled by a group composed of many minds, of either sex, both Schools of Buddhism and a dozen nationalities, it is the "common denominator" of many, often conflicting, points of view. Based though it is upon the Thera Vada point of view, it borrows from the Mahayana sufficient of its principles to make once more of the whole the complete philosophy for daily needs which the Buddha gave the world. Again, it is, though primarily written for the West, a demonstration to the Members of both Buddhist Schools that Truth, as always, is to be found in the balanced union of the two. It strives to be at once informative and a spur to individual study and experiment, on the one hand giving a comprehensive outline of the subject, on the other hand repeating what the Buddha taught his followers, that none can truly teach another—at the best he can but point the Way to self-enlightenment.

If, owing to the exigencies of space, some statements are presented in dogmatic form, it must be realised that Buddhism asks no man to believe, but merely to accept its principles as reasonable hypotheses until experience has shown them to be true.

Part II, which forms the substance of the book, has been arranged in the form of Question and Answer, the Enquirer being, we hope, a representative of the average cultured Westerner who genuinely seeks a solution to the problems which the religion of his fathers failed to solve.

The philosophy of Buddhism forms a connected whole and therefore it has proved difficult to resolve it into a reasoned argument, for it has, so to speak, no beginning and no end, but we think that such a form of exposition will appeal to the Western mind.

An intellectual understanding of Buddhism is, however, of little avail, for it must be lived before it can be truly known. Any man is entitled to reject its principles as not appealing to him, but only he who has tested them in daily life is competent to say, and none so testing them has ever said, they are not true.

Although the vast majority of men consider themselves as seekers after Truth, they are but few who welcome it when found. Prejudice, self-interest and mental laziness combine to make the average man prefer his comfortable illusions to the naked truth. Yet some there are who genuinely seek that Wisdom of which each religion and philosophy reflects a part, and will not rest until they find it.

To these strong-minded, fearless few the All-Enlightened One proclaimed the Dhamma of salvation by self-effort, and to such we dedicate this genuine attempt to present the West, in simple form, with the essence of his Teaching.

THE BUDDHIST LODGE, LONDON.

CONTENTS.

PART ONE.

THE LIFE OF THE BUDDHA.

Nothing we could say upon this subject would be original, and we are therefore confining ourselves to a brief outline and appending a list of books from which further knowledge may be obtained.

The Buddha has, as it were, two aspects, the one historic, the other symbolic and legendary.

The Historic Buddha.

The great Teacher known as the Buddha was born 600—550 B.C. (authorities differ as to the exact date), at Kapilavastu in the modern state of Nepal, on the northern bank of the Ganges. His parents, King Suddhodana, and his wife Maya, ruled over the Sakya clan, which was of Aryan blood and of the Kshatriyya, or warrior, caste. The young Prince was named Siddhartha Gautama, or Gotama, though after his Enlightenment other titles were bestowed upon him such as *Sakyamuni*, " Sage of the Sakyas," and *Tathagata*, " he who has thus attained the Goal (Nirvana)," culminating in the greatest title ever held by man, *Buddha*, the Enlightened One. He is said to have been of glorious beauty and early proficient in all manly games and exercises. The finest brains in the country were summoned for his education, but he rapidly surpassed them all. Brought up in his father's palace, he lived the splendid and luxurious life of a King's son and in due course married a neighbouring Princess, Yasodhara, by whom he had a son, Rahula.

His horoscope at birth foretold that he would never be content with earthly kingship, but would become a spiritual leader of his fellow-men. His father, fearing lest his only son should leave his throne without an heir, sought to distract his thoughts with sensuous enjoyment, but all in vain. Gradually the mighty intellect awakened to its destiny, and one night in the Palace garden the climax came. Sir Edwin Arnold in the "Light of Asia" has beautifully described the great resolve and great renunciation, how the purpose of his life became clear to him, the necessity of finding an escape from the wheel of suffering and of teaching it to his fellow-men. With this resolve he renounced his throne and riches, and with a last look at his sleeping wife and child went forth into the night, a homeless wanderer, to find salvation for the world. For many years he strove to gain from hermits and ascetics of all kinds the answer to his problem, patiently examining and testing the complicated systems of salvation which they taught, but none could lead him to the end of suffering. Finally he realised that nowhere in the world was wisdom and salvation to be found except within, and casting aside asceticism as being as useless as a life of luxury, he retired alone into the forest to seek within his heart that peace which is the end of suffering.

And so in the course of time there came to him as he sat in meditation under the Bodhi (Wisdom) Tree the culmination of lives of patient self-perfection and development. Deeper and deeper grew his spiritual insight into the nature of existence until, at the full moon of May at the age of thirty-five, the final fetter was broken and he attained supreme Enlightenment. Then came the great temptation. Of what avail to teach such depth of wisdom to a world fast set in selfishness and ignorance? On the other hand his all-embracing vision saw that there were some " whose eyes were scarcely covered with the dust of spiritual blindness, who would hear the Law," and he who had already surrendered all that men hold dear to find Enlightenment turned back upon the threshold of Nirvana that he might share his wisdom with all humanity.

For five and forty years he wandered over the length and breadth of Northern India, gradually forming round him the Buddhist *Sangha*, an Order of those who had renounced the world to find deliverance. Many of these he sent all over the East to spread the message of salvation by self-effort, while thousands came to him from distant parts to hear the Law. Finally, at the age of eighty, he passed away, explaining to his followers before he died that he was not leaving them, for " the Dhamma which I have given you, that shall be your Teacher when I am gone." And so, while Confucius and Lao Tze in China, and Pythagoras in Greece, were teaching in their respective spheres the principles of the Eternal Wisdom, Gotama, the wandering ascetic, by his own unaided efforts in innumerable lives, achieved the highest office in the human hierarchy and once more showed the Way which all may follow to that end.

In the course of years the Teaching was disseminated by the Brothers of the Order through Ceylon and Burma, China and Japan, Tibet, Korea, Mongolia and Siam, until to-day it is computed that one-third of the human race reveres the memory of an All-Compassionate One who, five hundred years B.C., proclaimed the Way that leads to the end of Suffering.

The Symbolic Buddha.

Fully considered as it is in several of the undermentioned books. there is no need to enlarge upon this aspect of the Buddha here. Suffice it to say that the inner teaching places Gotama as fourth in the present cycle of Buddhas of whom in æons past there have been many more. The next, or fifth of the present cycle, will not come for many thousands of years, when the Aryan race is drawing to a close, and even the face of the earth will be far different.

From this point of view the Buddha is a periodic incarnation of that Eternal Wisdom which in a mystic sense is to be found in the heart of every man. But whether he be loved as a man who gave up all to guide humanity from the snares of ignorance, or as a symbol of the Truth which dwells within, on Wesak Day throughout the world innumerable millions of men and women gather together at the nearest

Shrine to commemorate the birth, enlightenment and passing away of the greatest of the sons of men, Siddhartha Gotama, the All-Enlightened One.

SHORT LIST OF BOOKS ON THE LIFE OF THE BUDDHA.

The Light of Asia. Sir Edwin Arnold. Kegan Paul. Editions at all prices from 2/-. Written in verse. Most famous book on Buddhism in English.

The Life of Gotama the Buddha. E. H. Brewster. Kegan Paul. 1926. 10/6. A synthesis of extracts from the Pali Canon.

The Life of Buddha. Dr. N. J. Krom. Martinus Nijhoff. The Hague. 1926. 17/6. As depicted on the bas-reliefs on the stupa at Borabadur according to the *Lalitavistara* text. With 120 reproductions.

The Life of Buddha as Legend and History. Edward J. Thomas. Kegan Paul. 1927. 12/6. A scholarly analysis in the light of the higher criticism.

The Life of the Buddha. W. Woodville Rockhill. Kegan Paul. 1907. 10/6. As derived from the Tibetan Canon.

The Splendour of Asia. L. Adams Beck. W. Collins & Co. 1927. 7/6. Told as fiction, but based on the Scriptures.

Mysticism of East and West. Chapter 8. "The Buddha's Personality." William Loftus Hare. Jonathan Cape. 1923. 10/6.

Buddhism and Christianity. J. Estlin Carpenter. Hodder and Stoughton. 1923. 3/6. Particularly Chapter 3. An interesting comparison with Jesus.

Story of the Buddha. Edith Holland. Harrap. 2 net. For young people.

For further works, see Bibliographies contained in the above.

PART TWO.

THE TEACHING.

SECTION ONE.

What is Buddhism?

Question.—What is Buddhism?

Answer.—It is a Western term for the Teaching of the Buddha. It is known in the East as "the Buddha Dhamma," the word Dhamma being the Pali equivalent of the Sanscrit "Dharma."

Q.—And presumably one who studies these Teachings is a Buddhist?

A.—Not necessarily. A Buddhist may be defined as one who studies, disseminates and endeavours to live the fundamental principles of the Dhamma.

Q.—Are all three things necessary?

A.—They are. We must study before we can teach, but having studied it is our duty to live up to and to spread abroad such truths as we have learnt, for the benefit of those who know even less than we.

"Go ye now, Bhikkhus, and wander forth for the welfare of the many, out of compassion for the world. Let not two of you go the same way. Preach the Dhamma which is perfect in the beginning, perfect in the middle, perfect at the end, in the spirit and in the letter; proclaim a perfect life of holiness. There are beings whose mental eyes are scarcely covered with any dust, yet lacking because of not hearing the Dhamma . . . . they will understand the Dhamma." (*Mahavagga*:—*Vinaya I*, 21) (*Samyutta Nikaya*. Vol. I, p. 105.) But knowledge is useless unless and until it is applied, and the finest of all propaganda is that of personal example; therefore, while studying and teaching, we at the same time endeavour to embody the teaching in our daily lives. It is interesting to notice that in the East Buddhists call themselves "Followers of the Buddha," not merely students of the Dhamma.

Q.—Do you claim that this Dhamma is synonymous with Truth?

A.—No, we admit it to be a limited teaching, "to be used and then transcended," but we say of it, firstly, that it is the most complete and the most important religion yet known to man, and secondly, that it is a pre-requisite in one form or another to further and deeper knowledge of that Central Truth of which the Dhamma is but a partial expression.

Q.—But if it be only a fragment of Truth, may it not be that other religions and philosophies are also fragments of that Truth?

A.—We say they are. We say that all the great philosophies, religions and faiths now known to man, and others that once were known but now are forgotten, are each in their original form a partial expression of this mighty Truth. Yet would not their sum total represent the whole Truth, which can never be attained by men until by their own efforts they have reached Nirvana.

Q.—Then why do you say that Buddhism is the largest portion of this Truth now known to man?

A.—We cannot prove it, but we ask you to consider this summary of Buddhism as a religion, which is based upon an extract from The Bhikkhu Subhadra's "*Message of Buddhism*," page 84:

> Buddhism teaches the way to perfect goodness and wisdom without a personal God; the highest knowledge without a "revelation"; a moral world-order and just retribution, carried out of necessity by reason of the laws of nature and of our own being; continued existence without a separate "immortal soul"; eternal bliss without a local heaven; the possibility of redemption without a vicarious redeemer, a salvation in which everyone is his own saviour, and which can be obtained in this life and on this earth by the exercise of one's own faculties, without prayers, sacrifices, penances or ceremonies, without ordained priests, without the mediation of saints, and without Divine Grace.

Who else in history has proclaimed these doctrines, not merely to a chosen few, but to the whole world?

Q.—Others since the time of the Buddha have taught portions of these doctrines, if not the whole.

A.—Granted; but modern research tends to show the probability of the majority of religious teachers and philosophers since 500 B.C. as having been directly or indirectly influenced by Buddhist thought, from Pythagoras and Plato to Schopenhauer and Bergson, and from Jesus to Auguste Comte. Again, you will realise later on that not only is Buddhism the most in accord with modern science of all the religions and philosophies yet proclaimed, but that the whole trend of modern science is to prove the accuracy of the Buddha's analysis of phenomena. Finally it must be remembered that over one-third of the human race, through one form of Buddhism or another, looks to the Buddha as the Supreme Teacher of the Way to Enlightenment and Peace.

Q.—It seems, then, that as a system of thought Buddhism cannot be ignored in the search for Truth. But why do you call it a prerequisite for deeper knowledge?

A.—Before a child can understand the theories of an Einstein it must master the elements of mathematics. Before a man can understand the deeper Laws of the Buddha Wisdom he must first apprehend the nature of phenomena, including himself and the world as he sees it around him. Even this, as he sooner or later learns, involves sustained and concentrated thought.

Q.—But a rogue can do that as well as a Saint.

A.—He can, but that is all he will ever learn so long as he remains a rogue. Ethics and philosophy are inter-dependent. A system of ethics is of no lasting value unless based on philosophy, and knowledge is a dangerous asset unless founded upon sound morality.

Q.—Give me examples.

A.—As an example of the former, consider the precepts of morality inculcated in young people by a hundred organisations in the West. While in their Society they conform to the excellent standard set by its traditions, but on leaving it they tend to cast off the artificial moral support of its "herd-complex" or corporate tradition, and quickly fall to the level of their new surroundings. They lack an elementary knowledge of those Laws of Life we call philosophy, to form a basis for their somewhat parrot-like morality.

Q.—And as an example of your converse proposition, you are probably thinking of scientists and war?

A.—Exactly. A true scientist is, of course, solely concerned with the acquisition of knowledge, but there are scores of professing scientists in the West who dedicate their lives to applying their knowledge to the discovery of fresh ways of destroying their brother men. Why? Because their knowledge has outstripped their morality. Hatred, born of fear, is the motive of their efforts, even though it may be masked as patriotism, whereas the motive should be solely the welfare of Humanity.

Q.—But many scientists are working for humanity. What of medical research, for example?

A.—We grant that those of the type we have cited are in a minority, but their power is sufficient to wreck civilisation, and it *will*, unless, before it is too late, they learn to use their newly-found powers constructively rather than destructively. It is because the East has ever used its knowledge for the welfare of mankind that we seek to spread its doctrines in the West.

Q.—You say, then, that morality and philosophy must ever go hand in hand?

A.—We do. We say that only when an intellectual grasp of the basic principles of the Dhamma has been founded upon the bed-rock of moral integrity can a man with safety progress further towards the Truth.

Q.—Then sooner or later we must all be Buddhists?

A.—Within our definition, yes! But you will notice that it is the principles which matter, not the terminology or labels under which they may be learnt.

Q.—Your viewpoint is new to me, and some of your ideas are arresting. Let me have some further details of your religion.

A.—Let me first ask you what you mean by the word "religion," as I may not admit the accuracy of applying that word to Buddhism.

Q.—Surely the word is usually taken to mean a system of dogmas, ceremonies and observances calculated to bring about perfect alignment or harmony between the soul of the individual and his Creator, call Him what you will?

A.—If that be so, then Buddhism is not a religion, in that it knows nothing of dogmas necessary to be accepted on blind faith; nor of ceremonies conducive to salvation; nor of a

Creator to Whom such observances may be directed; nor of a soul which may be saved.

Buddhism and the "God" idea.

Q.—Then you are atheists?

A.—If by atheist you mean one who rejects the concept of a personal God, we are. But if you mean by that term one who entirely rejects the idea of a Reality or Noumenon behind phenomena, we are not. Therefore, if by the word religion you mean a way of thinking and a mode of life calculated to align the individual with the universal Law, then Buddhism is a religion. But in terms of present-day Western terminology it is safer to classify it as a Moral Philosophy, though, as will be seen later, even that description is inadequate. It is rather a philosophic discipline; a mode of life in conformity with a particular point of view.

Q.—But even a moral philosophy must deal with the relationship between the individual and God.

A.—So does Buddhism, but it analyses that complex collection of conflicting ideas comprised in the terms "God" with the same scientific accuracy with which it analyses the component factors of the notion "Man." The result of such analysis is to prove the current Western ideas on God, Soul and Man to be inaccurate and inadequate.

Q.—Then has Buddhism no doctrine corresponding to the Christian concept God?

A.—Certainly, but such doctrine is implicit in the Teachings of the Buddha, rather than expressed in terms.

Q.—Why? Surely it is fundamental?

A.—We agree: but for *practical reasons* the Buddha, on the subject of the Real, except for an occasional illuminating hint, "maintained a noble silence." If there *is* a Causeless Cause of all Causes, an Ultimate Reality, a Boundless Light, an Eternal Noumenon behind phenomena, it must clearly be infinite, unlimited, unconditioned and without attributes. We, on the other hand, are clearly finite, and limited and conditioned by, if not composed of, innumerable attributes. It follows that we can neither define, describe, nor usefully discuss the nature of That which is necessarily beyond the comprehension of our finite consciousness. It may be indicated by negatives and described indirectly by analogy, symbols and glyphs, but otherwise it must ever remain unknown and unexpressed, as being to us in our present state unknowable and inexpressible.

Q.—Then are such religions as postulate a personal God Who may be known by men, all based on fallacy?

A.—By no means, but it is a deep-rooted tendency of the human mind to attempt to drag the Infinite down to its own level, and to personify that which must ever remain an abstraction. Hence they themselves create a pale and distorted reflection of that Ultimate, Unchanging Reality, and worship it as God. Such anthropomorphic Deities may serve the purpose of the mentally immature, but will be rejected by every thinking man.

Q.—Why?

A.—Because the growth of human thought is from the personal and finite towards the impersonal and infinite.

Q.—But it is so much easier to think of the Supreme Spirit, call it what you will, as a person, even though logically the practice is absurd.

A.—We cannot help what is easier. The point is—What is true? Nor do we agree that the practice is easier. A growing mind can as easily digest the idea of a Universe guided by unswerving Law, as it can the concept of a distant Personage that it may never see, who dwells it knows not where, and who has at some time created out of nothing a Universe which is permeated by enmity, injustice, inequality of opportunity, and endless suffering and strife. Moreover, the practice is more than absurd; it is positively harmful.

Q.—How?

A.—Because in the hour of need he who believes in a personal God will instinctively appeal for help to this Power or Force as something outside himself, instead of calling up the strength that lies within. Not only does such a belief destroy self-reliance, but with it self-confidence, for this ruling Factor in his life must in its decisions, wishes and influence over him, ever remain to him unknown. Hence a spiritual slavery calculated to destroy self-confidence, self-reliance, and consequently self-respect.

Q.—In what, then, do you believe?

A.—The Buddhist sees around him a world which can be shown in all its parts to be impermanent and unreal. If all that we know is unreal, finite and transitory, logic demands the polar opposite in a Real which is both infinite and eternal. As a shadow needs its substance, as a reflection its object, so the provable unreality of Life as we know it necessitates an Ultimate Reality of which this Universe is the periodic and fleeting manifestation. " There is, O Bhikkhus, an unborn, unoriginated, uncreated, unformed. Were there not, there would be no escape from the world of the born, the originated, the created, the formed." (*Udana*, p. 112, and *Iti-Vuttaka*, p. 56).

Q.—Describe this Reality.

A.—We cannot. There is a saying: " If thou knowest the Uncreate, thou hast found deliverance." (Intro. *Udana* VI.) It is enough that reason, tradition and the intuition have ever been at one in refusing to admit this Wheel of Woe to be the answer to the Riddle of Life. All agree that there must be a Beyond, a changeless Silence and a Peace.

Q.—Is this Nirvana?

A.—Rather it is Parinirvana, that which is beyond Nirvana.

Q.—But surely the Buddha must have mentioned this Reality in his Teaching?

A.—Not directly, as far as his outer teaching for the people was concerned. " Just one thing do I teach," he said, " Suffering and Deliverance from Suffering." To the people he taught, save for occasional hints and passing allusions, nothing that could not be verified by the senses, or that was not a simple inference therefrom of immediate value in attaining liberation from the Wheel.

Q.—But he could have expounded the Truth as he knew it, and left his hearers to verify it for themselves as soon as the necessary faculties were evolved?

A.—Such was not his method in teaching the people. Again, at a time when India was filled with innumerable sects engaged in hair-splitting arguments on metaphysics, none of which was of immediate value in solving Life's problems, the Buddha's whole aim was to point out to men two things. First, the uselessness of idle speculation on matters incapable of proof or disproof, and which had no immediate bearing on the problem of emancipation, and secondly, the immediate necessity of finding, and of themselves using some means of escape from this "vale of tears" as the first step towards the direct knowledge of the deeper Wisdom which they sought. Had the Buddha added to their theories yet another of his own, which, though based on personal experience, could only be considered by his hearers as a theory incapable of proof, he would have helped them not at all. His whole aim was to lead their minds to practical considerations of self-development. "Just as, O Bhikkhus, the great ocean has but one taste, the taste of salt, so, O Bhikkhus, this Doctrine has but one taste, the taste of Deliverance" (*Udana*, p. 78). But even as a man may be given a railway ticket but must himself travel in the train, so must the seeker himself tread the Way to Liberation which the Buddha has so clearly pointed out. In brief. his Teaching was the clearly-expressed minimum which is the prerequisite for individual contact with the Buddha-Wisdom itself.

Q.—Then he taught nothing of the coming into being or ending of the Universe?

A.—To the people, no, for the reasons given above. But, as he was Buddha, "the fully Enlightened One," we may assume that he knew. "The Origin of the world, O Bhikkhus, and the Cessation of the world have been thoroughly understood by the Fully-Enlightened One, and have been realised by him" (Itivuttaka, 131).

Meanwhile he drew men's attention to matters of more immediate importance. He began with an analysis of Life as we know it, not with an account of a First Beginning which would be neither useful to, nor understood by his hearers.

Q.—The student, then, having by observation and deduction arrived at an intellectual grasp of Buddhism, what is his next step?

A.—To tread the Way for himself. Truth intellectually acquired has no influence over a man's conduct, as may be seen from many a so-called student of Buddhism or Christianity, and is therefore barren as a means of liberation from the Wheel. Wisdom cannot be obtained vicariously. Each must ultimately learn for himself, for even "Buddhas do but point the Way."

Q.—But knowledge is knowledge!

A.—True, but it is not Wisdom. Before

knowledge can be transmuted into Wisdom it must be tested in the crucible of daily life and slowly built into character. So, little by little, the seeker develops his own inner powers, until in time his consciousness merges into Wisdom itself, and he henceforth *knows*, as apart from believing, that Truth which the Buddha proclaimed might be known by all who choose to tread the age-long Middle Way. For the Supreme Wisdom itself can never be revealed to men. All that even a Buddha could say would be: "I have found the hidden Way to Truth and trodden it. That Truth is here before my eyes, for it is very part of me. I have proclaimed to all men how it may be found. Let those who weary of illusion follow in the selfsame Way."

Q.—Then is the whole Dhamma built up on lines of Western Science, from observed data to general principles?

A.—From one point of view it may be so considered. In terms of Western Philosophy it is derivable from *a posteriori* or inductive reasoning, that is, it may be arrived at intellectually by logical inference from an observed first premise.

Q.—Then presumably it has always existed, and the Buddha merely pointed out a logical process of thought by which its truth might be obtained?

A.—Say rather ratified. The Buddha asked his followers to believe nothing that could not be verified by the experience of the senses, and the simple inferences from knowledge so obtained. Buddhism is, therefore, very different from "Divine Revelation" in the sense of a series of dogmatic statements to be accepted on blind faith. Yet if by the word "revelation" be meant a re-pointing out of an ever-existing Way to Truth which had in time become obscured by human ignorance, then Buddhism is, if we may use the term, a re-revelation, for the Buddha repeatedly proclaimed that his mission was *once more* to point out the Way.

The Meaning of Dhamma.

Q.—You speak of the Way as contained in the Dhamma. What does the word mean?

A.—There is no equivalent English word. Many words have been suggested in translation, among them Law, Duty, the Good, the True, Righteousness or Right as opposed to wrong, the Norm, the Ideal, the Way, but it is the symbol of a concept of too complex a nature to admit of translation by any one English term. The basic idea is Form, in the English sense of "good form," or the conduct appropriate to any given occasion. It may be described as the outward manifestation of a body of Teaching, Moral Law, Doctrine, or system of philosophy, which has existed from all time in the abstract world of thought, which is Plato's "Noumenal Realm." Hence the meaning of Norm, or Ideal Form, as the clothing of a vast idea. But this Teaching carries its own punishment if disobeyed. Hence the saying "Vice, like Virtue, is its own reward." From this fact we get the aspect of the Dhamma as Law,—the Law of the Universe. This Law in turn, being universal in its application, represents Duty, or Right as opposed to wrong, that which all must perform if they would align themselves with, and not contend against the Law by which they live. For though "right" and "wrong" are from the human point of view relative terms, there is always, for any man at any given time "the proper thing to do." Finally, it bears the meaning of a Way or Approach to Truth. Hence an Eastern equivalent of the word Buddhism is Buddhagama, or "The approach to Enlightenment." To adopt Christian terminology—Dhamma is the outward and visible sign of an inward and spiritual Truth, and also the Way to its realisation.

Q.—I realise now how impossible it is to attempt to translate these Eastern philosophic terms into English.

A.—That is because the West, being essentially an unphilosophic civilisation, has no corresponding ideas for these Eastern terms, and no word is ever coined until it is necessary as the symbol of a thought.

Q.—You say that the Dhamma is built upon an observable first premise. But your description seems to imply a deliberate exposition by the Buddha of a portion of Wisdom in his possession, the whole of which he did not choose to disclose.

A.—Both propositions are true. An intellectual appreciation of the Dhamma may be obtained from scientific observation and inference, but it is in itself a partial exposition of that central Truth, a portion of which is taught to the world by the Founder of every great religion and philosophy, and hence can only be realised by a development of those latent faculties within by which Truth itself may be directly cognised.

But every Teacher must present Truth in a way that will be appropriate to his audience, and it is clearly better to lead one's hearers to an understanding of the Teaching by a process of logical inference from observable facts, than to lay down a collection of dogmatic statements and leave the individuals to prove their truth unaided for themselves.

Q.—I agree. Therefore I should like to know from what first premise this teaching may be deduced.

A.—Life—not in any technical sense, but in the ordinary acceptance of the term.

SECTION TWO.

The Characteristics of Existence.

Q.—Taking Life, then, as the starting point of Buddhist philosophy what do you say of it?

A.—We say that all forms of life can be shown to have three characteristics in common; impermanence, suffering, and an absence of permanent "soul" which separates each from every other form of life.

All is Impermanent.

Q.—I agree that most phenomena can be shown to be impermanent.

A.—The Buddha went farther. He pointed out how no single thing is the same at this moment as it was one moment ago. Even the "everlasting hills" are slowly being worn away by the wind and rain, and it is said that every particle of the human body, even the hardest, is replaced every seven years. The Christian echoes Buddhism and Science when he sings: "Change and decay in all around I see." There is no finality or rest within this Universe, only a ceaseless becoming and a never-ending change. As Shelley says: "Naught may endure but Mutability."

Q.—But presumably this change is itself subject to Law?

A.—Like all other natural processes it is cyclic. It is as an ever rolling wheel with four spokes—Birth, Growth, Decay and Death. Every form that comes into being goes through each stage in turn, and nought can stay the hand of time. The same applies to man-made objects and institutions. From a granite cathedral to a china vase, from a Code of Laws to an Empire: each and all rise to their zenith, and then as surely, however slowly, decay towards the inevitable end.

Thomas Gray put this well in his "Elegy written in a Country Churchyard":—

"The boast of heraldry, the pomp of power,
And all that beauty, all that wealth e'er gave,
Await alike th' inevitable hour:
The paths of glory lead but to the grave."

And again, Prospero in the Fourth Act of Shakespeare's "Tempest," says:—

"The cloud-capp'd towers, the gorgeous palaces,
The solemn temples, the great globe itself,
Yea, all which it inherit, shall dissolve
And, like this insubstantial pageant faded,
Leave not a rack behind. We are such stuff
As dreams are made on, and our little life
Is rounded with a sleep."

What lives must die, what began must end. "Impermanent are all component things."

All is Suffering.

Q.—That is so when one thinks of it. But why does this necessarily involve suffering?

A.—We now come to the central theme, the starting-point or basis of the Buddhist doctrine. You will agree that in the search for Truth we must face the facts of this scheme of things as we find them, even if we fain would "shatter it to bits, and then—remould it nearer to the Heart's Desire"?

Q.—Certainly.

A.—Very well, but we warn you that the result of such examination will be repugnant to your Western mind. The omnipresence of suffering or disharmony is a doctrine that can be grasped by the growing mind only when the hour is ripe. The fact that any individual proves incapable of understanding even a little of what it implies merely shows him to be not yet ready for escape from a condition of things with which he is quite content. Life is a school in which we have certain lessons to learn. Until they are learnt each pupil must remain. But there comes a time when

"Having tasted all
Experience, grown weary of desire
And fruitless pleasure, and as useless pain,
He turns his face from ways of worldliness
And sets out on the last long journey home."
("*The Conversion of the King.*")

Q.—Clearly we do not try to escape from a situation in which we are perfectly content, but I for one am not content with life as I know it, hence I seek those conditions under which it may be most comfortably borne.

A.—Your comfort will be but relative. The Buddha asked men to consider that "Birth is suffering, decay is suffering, disease is suffering, death is suffering. Union with the unpleasant is suffering, separation from the pleasant is suffering, and every craving that remains unsatisfied is suffering." (*Buddhist Suttas.* S.B.E. Vol. XI, p. 148.)

But note that the word "suffering" is only one English translation of the Pali word *Dukkha*, which includes all that we understand by pain, ill, disease—physical and mental—including such minor forms as disharmony, discomfort, irritation or friction, or, in a philosophic sense, the awareness of incompleteness or imperfection. It is dissatisfaction and discontent, the opposite of all that we mentally include in the terms well-being, perfection, wholeness, bliss. Taking the word in this sense, can you dispute the all-embracing dictum of the Buddha quoted above? Are not all the natural processes associated with suffering, and what have we gained in experience for which we have not paid in pain? "Suffering is common to all; life is a wheel and good fortune is unstable" (Phocylides).

Q.—Are you going to prove by reasoning alone that *Dukkha* is an integral factor in life?

A.—Let us try. Now you have agreed that nothing in this Universe is permanent, that all is in a constant state of flux. But where there is ceaseless change, there must also, in a world that is not mere machinery, but which is affected by the conflicting influence of countless decisions of the human will, of necessity co-exist disharmony and friction, with consequent irritation and discontent. We know that nothing can remain still for a single instant, and yet movement in any direction involves some measure, however slight, of pain.

Again, we have agreed upon an ultimate indescribable Reality of which this Universe is the periodic manifestation. Hence a duality, "Be-ness" as opposed to being, "Sistence" as opposed to *existence*, the Noumenon as opposed to phenomena. But duality is of necessity unstable, and all the mystics of the ages have agreed in yearning for a return to That from which they came. In the poetic imagery of Saint Augustine:
"For Thou, O Lord, hast made us of Thyself, and our hearts are ever restless 'til they find their rest in Thee."

There can be no abiding peace in a world of illusion.

From yet another point of view, the analogy of degree may help. Clearly disease is painful: but who is truly well? Old age gives rise to suffering, but age is a matter of degree, while adolescence knows the corresponding pangs of immaturity. Growing is as painful as dying.

Q.—But these forms of suffering are negligible.

A.—We repeat, it is all a matter of degree. Turn to the modern biological term for the impulse or urge that causes the lowliest forms of life, for example the amoeba, to search for con tact with something which may satisfy that urge, food. It is "irritability," which is the lowest form of desire. Yet the maxim holds "As above, so below." The Universe being homogeneous, every particle is a mirror of the whole. What applies to the amoeba applies to man. The basis of his every act is this "irritability" or desire, the satisfaction or absence of satisfaction of which alike gives rise to further suffering, as we shall see later.

If for the word "suffering" we substitute "imperfection," the same holds good in art. Art has been described as an attempt to portray permanence in impermanence, to manifest undying beauty in a perishable form. The impossibility of this alone spells imperfection, and the artist's inability to bring to earth more than a fraction of the "Beatific Vision" arouses in him a "Divine discontent" with all this world of form. For Reality alone is eternal, in its triple aspect of the Good, the Beautiful and the True.

Q.—All this, however, is mere reason and logic, undeniable perhaps, but hardly conclusive for a practical mind. Can you not help me to see with my own eyes the omnipresence of Dukkha?

By all means, if you will endeavour to keep an open mind and not be prejudiced by your Western upbringing, in which the pursuit of egoistic pleasure has played the most prominent part.

A.—Have you ever heard the story of the mustard seed?

Q.—No, tell it me.

A.—Once a distracted mother, Kisagotami by name, came to the All-compassionate One with her dead babe in her arms, and besought him that it might be restored to life. He listened to her pleading; then sent her to fetch a grain of mustard seed from a house where none had died. She sought for long,—in vain,—and then returned, and told him of the failure of her search.

"My sister! thou hast found," the Master said,
"Searching for what none finds—that bitter balm
I had to give thee. He thou lovedst slept
Dead on thy bosom yesterday: to-day
Thou know'st the whole wide world weeps with thy woe:
The grief which all hearts share grows less for one."

(Edwin Arnold's *Light of Asia*).

Such stories could be multiplied indefinitely, but of themselves they are of little avail. Either a man, on quiet consideration of life as he knows it, realises for himself the omnipresence of *Dukkha*, or he does not. In the latter event, if he prefers to consider things as different from what they are, his lesson has yet to be learnt. Sooner or later Time will teach it him.

But some there are whose lives are sufficiently unhappy for this truth to be all too apparent, or who have sufficiently withdrawn themselves from the appearance of happiness in their own or in their neighbours' lives to be able to hear, in the stillness of the night or above the turmoil of the day, the ceaseless cry of anguish that rises from a blindly groping, sorrow-laden world. To such, it is all too clear that as phenomena in a phenomenal world we are impermanent in all our parts and circumstances, and therefore are enmeshed in suffering.

Happiness.

Q.—Do you mean that we can never be happy, and that happiness itself, which is the goal of most human endeavour, is a foolish dream?

A.—Happiness is a word of many meanings, ranging from the purest bliss down to the drunkard's placid content at being temporarily free from care, but taking the word in its most usual meaning, consider this:—Life as we know it is expressed through millions of units, large and small, each striving towards its own ideal. But whether the end in view be good or bad, the interaction of such opposing ideals, ranging as they do from the purest altruism to the lowest form of selfishness, must inevitably cause constant friction and disharmony. Again, all effort, whether towards base or noble ends, involves a striving to become something different, something more, and this ceaseless "becoming-something-else" is in itself, as we have seen, productive of disharmony and discontent. Therefore, though a given individual may at a given moment consider himself happy, each one of the circumstances which compose that state of contentment is in a process of change; hence, the moment a change in any one of them disturbs the harmony of the whole, his "happiness" is ended.

Q.—Give me an example.

A.—The application of an abstract principle to a concrete example is never completely satisfactory as a means of making that principle clear, but consider the prosperous householder sitting in his garden on a summer's morn. On what does his happiness depend? On the weather; his health; the health, physical and mental, of his wife and of his children; his business prosperity, with all the factors that such a state of things implies, and a thousand other details you may set down for yourself. Yet when, as *must* happen sooner or later, any single one of these factors changes for the worse, he will be faced with *dukkha* in a proportionate degree. But suppose any one unit of life succeeds in achieving "happiness," can all the teeming millions of the earth's inhabitants achieve it simultaneously? Yet Life is one, and though the forms may vary, the Life within that suffers is the same in each. Hence the suffering of one is the suffering of all, even as the joy of one is the joy of all. That being so, how can any one being rest content while his brother's life is filled with suffering?

Q.—But happiness has been defined as "harmonious reaction to one's environment."

A.—Accepting that definition we reply that so long as our environment, which for a Buddhist embraces all that lives, is filled with suffering, our reaction to it can only be harmonious by a deliberate selection of pleasant environment, with a corresponding deliberate exclusion from our consciousness of the existence of the suffering of others.

Q.—Then no Buddhist seeks for happiness?

A.—Not as men usually understand the term. The happiness that most men seek is a fool's paradise, a temporary condition of self-induced *mâyâ* or illusion, a halting by the wayside to pluck the poisoned fruits of self, in that it can only be obtained by selfishly ignoring the hopeless misery of our fellow men.

Q.—Then our very efforts to find happiness for ourselves prevent us finding it?

A.—That is so. Selfish happiness is at the best temporary, and its exclusive, separative nature reacts in time as pain. True happiness, as has been pointed out by all the great Teachers of whom we have record, and as may be proved by all who care to test it for themselves, is only to be found in ceaseless altruistic effort on behalf of suffering mankind. As Shelley says:—

> "For when the power of imparting joy
> Is equal to the will, the human soul
> Requires no other heaven."
>
> (*Queen Mab.*)

Even then his happiness is only relative, nor can it ever be complete until the wailing cry of "the great orphan" humanity is silenced in Nirvana.

Q.—Yet some of the more successful in life seem to be perfectly happy?

A.—They may seem to be, but are they? Are the idle, selfish rich at ease with all their luxury, or does the useless burden of possessions cause them greater misery than a poorer brother ever knew, who faced his empty future with a smile and shared the little that he had with others still less fortunate than he? For it is we ourselves who create our happiness or woe. Just as the law of Karma, of cause and effect, creates our circumstance, so our reaction to that circumstance decides our peace of mind, and that reaction is controllable by the human will. As Epictetus said, "If any man be unhappy, let him know it is by reason of himself alone," for happiness depends, as your definition points out, not on our position in life, but on our attitude towards it, whatever it may be. Thus, for example, as Epictetus elsewhere says, "Wherever a man is against his will, that to him is a prison. Thus Socrates was not in prison since he was there with his own consent." A rich man's happiness depends on the use to which he puts his wealth, that is, on his "reaction to his environment." The same applies to the way in which a poor man faces his poverty and uses what little possessions he has.

Q.—I think I see what you mean, though at first sight it seems inconsistent. Life being one, we can never be perfectly happy until all are as happy as we are, but the nearest approach to perfect happiness is to be found in trying to remove the unhappiness of others?

A.—That is so.

Q.—Then the pursuit of happiness is permissible so long as it be sought in the proper way?

A.—If sought in the wrong way it will never be found, for selfishness is essentially separative and exclusive, and, as such, is an offence against the One Life. Hence the futility of seeking happiness for oneself at the expense of one's fellow-men.

Q.—Then is pleasure equally a delusion?

A.—All experience is either obviously unpleasant or apparently pleasant. But wherein lies the difference? Is pleasure pleasure, or is pleasure gilded pain? As Drummond says: "Earth's sweetest joy is but disguised pain," and Shelley says that "our sincerest laughter with some pain is fraught," and refers to "that unrest which men miscall delight."

Q.—This seems a very gloomy philosophy.

A.—It may be to the Western mind, for the West still tends towards individual struggle for individual happiness, instead of co-operative effort for the commonweal. It too often follows that the cost at which this happiness is purchased is a matter of no importance, even if it involve the misery and degradation of one's fellow men. Is it gloomy to condemn such happiness as this?

Q.—Presumably then no Buddhist will ever be seen to smile?

A.—On the contrary, those who walk through life with gloomy faces, striving to banish laughter from the world, mistake the half truth for the whole, for "though Sorrow be the portion of the night, Joy cometh in the morning," and Joy is the Song of the Universe, as far removed from selfish happiness as passion is from Love. The paradox is true that though this life be filled with suffering, and the Way that leads from suffering is itself a Path of pain, yet those who tread it do so in unutterable joy. Thus was Epictetus a true Buddhist in this respect, speaking of whom Hastings Crossley says:—"While retaining the grandeur of Stoic severity, he alone is distinguished by the gay and cheerful humour with which he would persuade men that the paths of renunciation and endurance are paths of pleasantness and peace." This "Holy Way" is one of the Buddhist meditations, and corresponds to the Christian idea of "Rejoice without ceasing, and again I say unto you, Rejoice." Such joy is no mere superficial happiness, but springs from the intuitive perception of the Universal Self within.

Is Buddhism Pessimistic?

Q.—But in spite of this the whole doctrine of *Dukkha* seems to me very pessimistic, a doctrine of despair!

A.—Whether we dislike the face of Truth or welcome her the Truth remains the same, and if this doctrine of Dukkha be not true the world has waited long to hear its falsity proclaimed. But Buddhism is neither pessimistic nor optimistic. Both are extremes, and in all things the Buddha proclaimed the Middle Way. As Professor Bosanquet says: "I believe in optimism, but I add that no optimism is worth its salt that does not go all the way with pessimism and arrive at a point beyond it." ("Social and International Ideals," p. 43). As J. E. Ellam wrote: "It is a perfectly natural trait in human nature that we should turn away from the disagreeable and thrust it out of sight. It is far more pleasant to dwell in a fool's paradise than in a wise man's purgatory. But the truly wise man . . . seeks to see life as it is, and to see it *whole*." (Buddhist Review, Vol. XI, p. 181.

Before we can escape from suffering we must face its existence and analyse its cause—desire. Such are the first two of the Four Noble Truths and as such they are pessimistic, but in Buddhism " there is no resignation to a common inevitable doom. The natural instinct to avoid pain and to make for its opposite is encouraged," though " particular painful experiences are to be patiently endured." (Mrs. Rhys Davids, "Buddhism" p. 162.)

Q.—Then we can escape from Suffering?

A.—" This above all do I teach," said the Buddha, " Dukkha and Deliverance from Dukkha." If the omnipresence of Dukkha and the nature of its cause, desire, be pessimistic, surely the Teaching of the Way to Liberation from Samsara, the Wheel of Rebirth, and the clear pronouncement that each and all may tread that Way and by his own efforts reach the self-same Goal, displays the noblest optimism yet proclaimed to Man? There is here no patronising and invidious choice, no separation of humanity into the " saved " and the " damned," only the pointing out of the age-long road by which each man may by his own efforts attain to freedom from the Wheel.

Q.—Nevertheless, Buddhism seems to advocate a supreme contempt for this life, about whose beauty and glory all the poets of the world have ever sung!

A.—Have they? Or have they sung of the glory of that transcendent Reality whose triple aspects they have worshipped as the Good, the Beautiful, and the True? It is of the presence of the Eternal in the temporary, the Real in the unreal that the poets have written, not of this fretful fever Life. As Lakshmi Narasu points out: "Life for its own sake is not worth living. Mere quantity of life without quality stands self-condemned. A life worth living is one that is full of active aspiration for something higher and nobler, full of . . . earnest devotion to the good of others," such life, in fact, as tends to lead men "from the unreal to the Real, from darkness to the Light, from death to Immortality." Mrs. Rhys Davids has well expressed this idea when she says, "Buddhism enhances, perhaps more than any other creed, the value of life, when life is taken not in breadth and length," but for some "special quality," that of depth, an inner realisation of the transitory nature of phenomena, and we suggest by inference, of the presence of, and of our oneness with, that Noumenon compared with which this life is of the substance of a dream.

For "is it not true that inward peace, though it can transfigure earth and make it beautiful, is won by detachment from earth, not by devotion to it?" (Edmond Holmes, *Creed of Buddha* p. 48.) It is not life that is evil but a foolish cleaving to life, a binding of oneself more tightly on the Wheel.

Q.—Buddhism is, therefore, a philosophy of suffering?

A.—It has been so described. If life is filled with suffering, and if suffering is the means by which we learn the lessons we are here to learn, is it not foolish to attempt to run away from School? Rather should we suffer gladly that we may become free, and thereby gain an inner poise and self-detachment from our own suffering by doing all we can to alleviate that of others; for while sorrow, like a clinging creeper, winds itself about the heart of man, the pursuit of earthly pleasure is an idle dream.

Q.—But one can dwell too much on the omnipresence of Dukkha.

A.—The Bhikkhu Silacara answers your question when he says: "There is a reason for the reiteration of the truth of suffering. That it is an extreme view may be granted, yet it is absolutely necessary to counterbalance the other equally extreme view, so that from the opposition of the two a juster equilibrium may result." (*Buddhist Review*, Vol. XI. p. 181.) For although the doctrine of *Dukkha* is, taken by itself, "an extreme view," it provides, when considered in conjunction with the complementary doctrine of Deliverance, a philosophy that is all-sufficient for the immediate needs of men.

Q.—But why should Buddhism be the only religion that harps so much on suffering?

A.—Because the object of the Buddha's teaching was to make man realise that life is something to be transcended rather than "enjoyed," and to show them how this might be done. To this end it was necessary to point out the unpleasant nature of their plaything, Life, before leading them on to something worthier of their attention. No man can be released from the Wheel of Rebirth until he realises he is bound upon it, for none can save another from illusion; each must ultimately liberate himself. Hence the first step was to lead men to a calm examination of the facts, and then to show to such as yearned for freedom how that freedom was to be attained. But all religions have recognised the omnipresence of suffering, though "it is Buddhism alone that made it the point of departure for its practical philosophy." (Mrs. Rhys Davids, *Buddhism*. p. 159.) For instance, not only in the New Testament, but also among the leading modern Churchmen, is the doctrine of *dukkha* held. As an example of the latter we cannot do better than quote Canon Streeter, who is recognised as one of the leading metaphysicians of the Church of England. In his work "*Reality*" at page 57, he says: "Pain is the fundamental fact in Life. Wherever Life is there is Pain." But as Dr. Estlin Carpenter points out in *Buddhism and Christianity* at page 62: "Christianity can never explain suffering." Lacking the idea of causality, which is one of the basic doctrines of Buddhism, the Christian must needs hold that suffering comes from the Will of the Creator, for if man be created by God he can have no choice or decision in his own creation, nor in that of the surroundings into which he is born. Hence, as the cause of suffering is God, man is quite powerless to remove that cause. Not so in Buddhism, as we shall see later.

All is Anatta.

Q.—So much, then, for Anicca—Impermanence, and Dukkha. which is suffering in all its forms. What is the third Characteristic of Life?

A.—Anatta, the doctrine that nothing in existence has within it a permanent "soul" or imperishable entity that distinguishes it from other forms of life.

Q.—I understand that this is a very difficult idea to grasp.

A.—This is mainly due to the somewhat mechanical and materialistic viewpoint of certain writers of the Theravada or Southern School. We will discuss later the comparative viewpoint of these two Schools of Buddhism, but for the moment we will merely state that our own view, supported we claim by the Pali scriptures, is nearer to that of the Northern or Mahayana School. The true Buddhist teaching concerning the soul is, we think, clearly stated by Dr. McGovern when he says: "Buddhism insists that the soul is not a rigid, unchanging, self-constituted entity, but a living, complex, changing, evolving organism." (*Intro. to Mahayana Buddhism*, p. 132.)

Q.—What, then, is this doctrine of Anatta?

A.—It is the opposite of the doctrine of Atman, or Atta, as generally understood by the Brahmins at the time when the Buddha was teaching, for this Atta doctrine was of two kinds, the original and the degraded forms.

Q.—What was the original?

A.—The philosophy of the Upanishads, on which the Vedanta, or Brahmin philosophy, was based, proclaims that Life is One. At the heart of the Universe is the One Reality of which the Universe as we know it is but a periodic manifestation. This is the only Supreme Deity known to Indian thought, for the Upanishad philosophy, like Buddhism, "revolts against the deistic conception of God." (*Philosophy of the Upanishads*, Radhakrishnan, p. 79.)

But as the finite can never return to the Infinite unless it is in essence one with that Infinity, so there is behind rather than in each man and all that lives " the divine element which we call the beatific consciousness, the ananda state, by which at rare moments it enters into immediate relations with the Absolute." (Ibid. p. 80.)

This element is called the Atman or Atta, and the quintessence of Indian thought may be summed up by saying that this Atman of man and the Atman of the Universe are one. As Mr. Holmes says in his introduction to the same work (p. 4), " The Upanishads are dominated by one paramount conception, that of the ideal oneness of the soul of man with the soul of the universe," and the same recurrent theme will be found to form the spiritual basis of ethics and the beginning and end of all mysticism.

But this doctrine, which, under different terminology, is that of the Mahayana School, was gradually degraded into the belief in an " immortal soul " as that part of man which distinguished and separated him from all other forms of life, whereas in truth this Atman, or " Spark of the Divine " is not the " soul " at all, though often loosely described as such, for " it is no 'human' but the universal *absolute* principle " which is common to and unifies man and the Universe, as H. P. Blavatsky points out. (*Key to Theosophy*, p. 93.)

Therefore, not only is this Atman not that which distinguishes man from man, but it is actually that element which is the "common denominator" of all forms of life, and is hence the philosophic basis of the Brotherhood of Man. The degradation of this noble idea is paralleled in modern Christianity, in which the self-same teaching of St. Paul has been caricatured in the conception of an "eternal soul" which distinguishes each man from his neighbour, and which will be either "saved" or "damned" at death according as the preponderance of his deeds in one short life is good or bad. It was against *this* belief, called by him the *Heresy of Separateness*, that the Buddha so strenuously inveighed.

Q.—Then you accept the existence of this "Atman"?

A.—In its original sense, yes. But it is not an entity, nor is it in man. It is the Universal Principle, manifesting as the One Life, which shines through every form of life from mineral to man. But as Buddhists we do not accept the permanent, immortal soul as found in the Brahmin philosophy at the time of the Buddha, and in Christianity to-day.

What is "Soul"?

Q.—But I have seen the word *Anatta* translated as "soullessness."

A.—We agree with Allan Bennet that those who do so "convey a totally wrong idea, seeing how much of the highest and noblest in our Western thought is bound up with the word soul" (*Wisdom of the Aryas* p, 57.) The Buddha nowhere denies the Atman doctrine as originally taught, but only in the degraded form of an "immortal soul" which separates man from man. It is true that in his "*Buddhism in Translations*" Mr. Warren has collected a series of extracts from the Pali Canon, and headed them, "There is no Ego," but as Mr. Holmes points out (*Creed of Buddha*, p. 168). "Not a word is said in disproof of the existence of the Ego. The point of the argument (in each case) is that each of the apparent Egos—of form, of sensation, and the rest—is unreal," that is, that none of the factors that collectively form what we know as man, consisting of body, sensation, perceptions, etc., is in itself permanent, nor are they so collectively, but each and all are in a constant state of flux. Thus, not only is there no denial of the Atman, but there is no denial of the soul of man as something "capable of growth, as of deterioration, changing according to the nature of its deeds for better or worse," as Plato said: this is not the aspect of animism rejected by Buddhism." (Mrs. Rhys Davids' *Buddhism*, p. 141).

Q.—But did the Buddha expressly affirm the existence of such "soul"?

A.—No more than he denied it, but any attempt by him to explain the intricacies of such a complex problem as the nature of self to those whose chief fault lay in their love of discussing metaphysical detail instead of applying fundamental principles, would have been of no assistance to them in attaining liberation from the Wheel. Hence, beyond denying that those who said "There is a self," were any more correct than those who said, "There is no self," the

Buddha, as always on such subjects, "maintained a noble silence."

Our only reason for presuming to give a brief explanation of this and other subjects on which, in his teaching to the multitude, the Buddha chose to remain silent, is that in order to refute what we believe to be the utterly wrong view of the West, we must replace the doctrine we consider wrong with that which we consider right, but we warn you that the subject being essentially metaphysical is a difficult one for the Western mind to grasp, and needs a determination to assimilate the idea, and not to stumble at our choice of words.

Q.—I will try. Then it was not against the existence of a soul or self, but against the wrong conceptions of its nature that the Buddha rebelled?

A.—That is so. We believe that Lakshmi Narasu expresses the true teaching when he says (*Essence of Buddhism*, p. 302.): "That which is called the ego, which says 'I am,' is merely an aggregate of *skandhas*, a complex of sensations, ideas, thoughts, emotions and volitions. It is not an eternal immutable entity behind these. The word 'I' remains the same, but its significance continually changes." The maxim holds: "Impermanent are *all* component things." In a universe in which all forms of life are fragments of an Indivisible Unity, if such a paradox be understood, the fact that each is clothed in the temporary garments of matter does not make those garments or any of them separate the true man from the Whole of which he is a part. Hence is the Doctrine of

Anatta described as that of "non-independence," and is therefore inferentially the Buddhist recognition of the Brotherhood of Man as an already existing fact in nature, and not merely as a beautiful ideal. Herein lies the distinction between Christianity and Buddhism, for in the former "each single individual stands to his Creator as an independent solitary soul; but in Buddhism each soul is not only related as such to the highest reality, but also to one another in the most perfect network of infinite mutual relationship." (*Suzuki*, *The Eastern Buddhist*, Vol. 4, p 77.)

For in Buddhist eyes,

> "All Life is One. The woods, the open sky,
> Man, and the humblest insect on the wall,
> And everything that is, share in a way
> Most wonderful to those who understand,
> A common heritage."

(*The Conversion of the King*, p. 12.)

Q.—What is the relation of this doctrine of *Anatta* to that of *Dukkha*?

A.—It is through non-recognition of the Buddhist standpoint that man experiences greater suffering than is involved in the mere fact of existence.

"Life's long enduring suffering has arisen out of the blind Nescience of itself as One . . . out of the non-recognition by Life of its underlying unity of purpose and of aim." (*Wisdom of the Aryas*, p. xxi.) Prof. Rhys Davids foreshadowed the above when he said (*Buddhism*, Putnam, p. 124), "Sorrow is in fact the result of the effort which an individual has to make to keep separate from the rest of existence," and again, " Such states of mind as coexist with the consciousness of individuality, with the sense of separate existence, are states of suffering." *Buddhism*, S.P.C.K., p. 48.) So much for the sorrow which is inherent in all manifestation by virtue of the fact of Anicca. With regard to the suffering caused by men, is not this too caused by ignorance of Anatta, ignorance of the fact that Life is one, and that the gain or loss, sorrow or joy of one, is that of all?

Q.—Then in spite of obvious differences between Buddhism and Christianity, you seem to agree with the " Body, Soul and Spirit " of St. Paul?

A.—The Mahayana or Northern School certainly does, and the Theravada School nowhere denies it. There are three things to be considered.

1.—Spirit or Atman, which is the " common denominator " of all forms of Life, and is the monopoly of none. This alone is Eternal, but it is not an immortal entity, for " there is no abiding principle in man."

2.—Soul, in the sense of a growing, evolving bundle of attributes or characteristics, forming character. This it is that reincarnates from life to life on the long road to perfection: this it is to which Mrs. Rhys Davids refers as " the convenient, not to say necessary notion whereby we speak of ourselves as " I " or a " self." (*Buddhism*, p. 54.)

3.—Body, used in the sense of " personality," composed of all the attributes or " skandhas " which we will examine later. In the Northern

School, as in the true Brahmin philosophy and elsewhere, these three "principles" are subdivided into six or seven, according as Atman is regarded as a human principle or not, but the above triple division serves our present purposes. The point to be made clear is that there is nothing in man that entitles him to say "I am this and you are that" through all Eternity. It is this "Heresy of Separateness" that is the cause of the almost incredible selfishness of the West, for once establish that "I" am utterly different, separate from "You," and fratricidal wars in trade, politics, and in the open field will follow as a matter of course. Above the clamour of competitive strife the self-same Teaching of the Christ remains unheard.

Q.—You spoke of the Southern School's materialistic attitude?

A.—In disclaiming the existence of a separate, immortal soul, some scholars of the Theravada went too far, and presumed to interpret the Buddha's silence concerning the self as denying the whole Atta doctrine in its original form, and with it the evolving soul. Not only are there no grounds for so sweeping an abolition of the accumulated wisdom of the ages, but such an attitude has placed the Theravada scholars in a philosophical position which no amount of specious argument can overcome. For if the five "skandhas" mentioned above are the whole of man's heritage, what is the meaning of such phrases in the Scriptures as "Self is the Lord of self" (Dhammapada), and what is the meaning of self-reliance and self-control? But if the evolving soul be taken as the reservoir of character brought over from life to life, or, which is the same thing, as the resultant of the effects of past causes, we have an entity, growing, changing, and therefore impermanent as a separated self, but none the less for the time being a thing, which gradually learns to control its vehicles, the skandhas. This it is that having by an age-long process of self-purification won to freedom, " knows that it is free," and casting aside the last of the Ten Fetters that bound it to the wheel of rebirth, enters Nirvana.

Q.—Then what is the relation of this " soul " to spirit?

A.—Reunion with the latter is the goal of the former, for ultimately when the weary Pilgrimage is over we shall finally cast aside the last of those various " personalities " whose usefulness as an instrument for acquiring knowledge will be over, and the perfected Ego or Soul, being free from all impurity will become one with that spark or " Ray of the Absolute," Atta, when " the dewdrop slips into the Shining Sea."

That is all that can be usefully said here on the subject of Atta and Anatta. The eye of intuition is needed to understand those paradoxes by which alone the highest truths can be expressed in words, which explains why the Buddha refused to dilate upon such matters to an audience of intellectual wranglers (as most of the finest intellects in India then were), but rather pointed out the Path by which in time they might develop in themselves the necessary faculties for cognising Truth at first hand. Of the nature of man we will say more later, but it will now be clear that in all his parts he is, like all else in existence, subject to impermanence, filled with suffering and discontent, and lacking any element which eternally distinguishes him from other forms of Life.

SECTION THREE.

The Four Noble Truths.

Q.—What is the next step in your exposition of Buddhism?

A.—In the course of his forty-five years of teaching the Buddha is reported as having again and again laid down what he considered to be the essential philosophy of everyday life, and this epitome he called the Four Noble Truths. Other systems of philosophy have given accounts, necessarily incomplete, of various aspects of that body of truth we call the Buddha-Wisdom, but the distinctive feature of the Buddha's teaching was his unwillingness to give his hearers any further material for argument on subjects which the intellect alone could never understand. He preferred to point out how the Truth itself might be attained by every man by the slow development of the latent faculties within.

Once, when two venerable Sages were discussing the Buddha's teaching, the first one, Sariputta, asked: "Does the Tathagata exist beyond death?" "That," replied the other, Kassapa by name, "is undeclared." The same answer was given to the questions: "Does then the Tathagata not exist beyond death, or both exist and not exist, or neither exist nor not exist?" Asked why this information was undeclared, Kassapa replied: "These questions are unprofitable . . . are not concerned with the first principles of the holy life . . . do not conduce to calm, to supernormal wisdom, nor to Nirvana. But this has been declared by him:—That this is Suffering; that this is the Cause of Suffering; that this is the End of Suffering; that this is the Way that leads to the End of Suffering. . . . This conduces to calm, to supernormal wisdom, to Nirvana."

This story applies to most of those problems on which the mind of man has ever sought enlightenment, the answer to which, however, even if apparently found, would be of little or no service to the finder in gaining liberation from the Wheel. The futile dialectics of the Churchmen of the Middle Ages afford an interesting parallel. Throughout his whole long life the Buddha consistently proclaimed that none could save his brother from the Wheel. The final Truth can never be revealed to men, but each must ultimately find it for himself. Hence his advice to set about the search without delay. The Way thereto was pointed out, but each would have to tread it for himself. It is as though a man sought knowledge of a certain city, and by much questioning of learned men and poring over books he found out this and that. And then the Buddha was consulted, who replied: "See, Brother, yonder lies the city, and here before you lies the Way. Tread that Way and you will find it for yourself: none hinders you."

Again, in the Majjhima Nikaya (I. Chap. 63) the Buddha gives a graphic description of such men as wander in the maze of dialectics heedless of the fact that with all their intellectual brilliance they were none the less fast bound upon the Wheel. "Suppose a man were pierced with a poisoned arrow and his friends were to summon a surgeon. And suppose that man were to say: 'You may not pull out the arrow until I know whether the man who shot it is of this clan or that; whether tall or short; whether the bow was long or short and the bow-string made of this or of that'; . . . that man would die, but still these matters would not be found out by him. Just so is he who says: 'I will not listen to the All-Enlightened One until I know whether the world be eternal or not, whether the Tathagata exists beyond death or not'; . . . such an one would die but would not learn these things. But I declare that whether these things are so or not, there is suffering, grief, despair, and of these things I teach the end." (*Some Sayings of the Buddha.* Woodward, p. 305.) In other words, a profound understanding of these Truths, and a faithful treading of the Noble Eightfold Path is the only way in which the Truth may be known in all its purity.

Q.—Then what are those truths?

A.—The first is one of the Three Signs of Being—SUFFERING. "Which, O Bhikkhus, think you is the greater; the tears which you have poured out, wailing and lamenting on this long pilgrimage . . . joined to the unloved, separated from the loved; or the waters of the Four Great Seas?" (*Samyutta Nikaya*).

Such is the disease that needs a Buddha's curing, and the diagnosis of the All-Enlightened One proclaimed its cause to be desire, the never-ending craving of the senses, the selfish grasping of the "lower self," indifferent to the needs and claims of others, the thirst for sentient existence. But a cure for the disease has been discovered and a prescription given and applied. If the first two truths be pessimistic, the third and fourth are as trumpet calls to those who "travail and are heavy laden," for they proclaim the End of Suffering by the elimination of its cause, desire, accomplished by the treading of the Eightfold Path.

Q.—This, then, is the kernel of the Buddhist philosophy?

A.—It is the ultimate minimum that each must understand. Even if a man knows nothing of such questions as the nature of the self or of the Universe, of the life after death, or what it is that is reborn, it is no matter, for of these things the Buddha said: "This question is not calculated to profit, to perfect calm, to supernormal wisdom, to Nirvana." But let a man realise to the full these four great propositions and he will need nothing more, for whereas human knowledge is, at the best, composed of fragments of the Truth, the Noble Eightfold Path is, as we have said, a way to Truth itself. Therefore, the sooner these truths are learnt the sooner will each sufferer be free, for it is "through not understanding, through not penetrating the Four Aryan Truths, O Bhikkhus, that we have wandered round this long, long journey, you and I." (Digha Nikaya 2, 90, P.T.S. Ed.)

Desire.

Q.—What exactly is included in the word "desire"?

A.—Just as " suffering " is but a partial and somewhat misleading translation of *dukkha,* so " desire," unless explained, is hardly an accurate translation of the Pali term *tanha* (in Sanskrit *trishna*), for desire appears in many forms, ranging from ungovernable lust to the purest yearning for the helping of mankind.

Tanha means in the first place that craving which supplies the binding force to hold men on the Wheel of Rebirth, its nearest Western equivalent being " the Will to Live."

" Verily it is this thirst or craving, causing the renewal of existence, accompanied by sensual delight, seeking satisfaction now here, now there —the craving for the gratification of the passions, for continued existence in the worlds of sense. (*Buddhist Suttas.* S.B.E. Vol. XI, p. 148.) Or, as Rhys Davids points out in his comment, paraphrasing the Christian summary—" The lust of the Flesh, the lust of Life, and the love of this present world."

For the passional element of this desire, the word *Kama* is generally used, and in this latter sense desire is associated with temptation, as is shown by a Chinese version of this Second Noble Truth which is " the assembling of temptation."

In brief, desire means those inclinations which tend to continue or increase separateness, the separate existence of the subject of desire; in fact all forms of selfishness, the essence of which is desire for self at the expense, if necessary, of all other forms of life.

Q.—But why do you say that this desire is the cause of suffering?

A.—Because all that tends towards separateness is contrary to the Law of the Universe which tends towards harmonious co-operation between its parts. Again, Life being one, all that tends to separate one aspect from another must needs cause suffering to the unit that even unconsciously works against the Law. Man's duty to his brothers is to understand them as extensions, other aspects of himself, as being fellow facets of the same Reality. The Stoic Emperor Marcus Aurelius discovered this when he advised his readers to "Enter into each man's Inner Self, and let all others enter into thine."

Again, from the viewpoint of the individual, are not most of the "ills that flesh is heir to" caused by thwarted personal desire? What is disappointment but desire unsatisfied? From what does anger usually spring if not from the action of another that is contrary to one's wish, and whence come worry and anxiety if not from the fear that things will not fall out as we would have them, were they subject to our will? But slay the desires of self and "learn to wish that all shall come to pass exactly as it does" and there will ensue that calm, unutterable peace of mind which only comes when self, the lower separated self, is dead. "To-morrow my business will prosper, or it will not, my friend will recover, or he will not, I shall receive the reward of my labours in regard to this or that, or I shall not." What then? To a philosopher these things are of no importance.

Q.—But this is blind fatalism!

A.—By no means. It is a man's duty to do the work in hand to the best of his ability, but his workmanship is in no way enhanced by fretful desire for recognition, or constant anxiety as to the nature of the result. If the latter is under his control, let him do all he can towards making it as he would have it be; if it is not, surely it is foolish of him to waste emotion on an outcome over which he has no control. Until humanity can consciously control its destiny, to desire, from whatever motive, that events should fall out in this way or in that is waste of time, while such desires as aim at purely selfish ends are as foolish as the million millionth part of a vast united Whole striving to attain its own ambition in defiance of the unconsulted millions that remain. All Life is One, and what is unselfishness, the greatest of all virtues, but a calm indifference to personal concerns so long as others be assisted to the best of one's ability? It follows that it is the never-ending cry of " I want this " and " I want that " that is the greatest cause of man-made suffering.

Of desire as a cause of rebirth we will speak later.

Q.—Then you do not teach the crushing out of nobler aspirations and ideals?

A.—By no means. As Prof. Radhakrishnan says, speaking of "desire" in Brahmanism; "even the ideal sage has desires, but they are not selfish desires. . . . *Kama* is only the animal desire; lust, the impulsive craving of the brute man. Desire as such is not forbidden. The desires for salvation and knowledge are commended. A distinction is drawn between true desires and false." (Philosophy of the Upanishads, p. 91.) " It is the desire for what belongs to the unreal self that generates suffering, for it is . . . impermanent, changeable, perishable, and that in the object of desire, causes disappointment, disillusionment, and other forms of suffering to him who desires. . . . Desire in itself is not evil. . . . It is desire to affirm the lower self, to live in it, cling to it, identify oneself with it, instead of with the Universal self that is evil." (Edmond Holmes, *Creed of Buddha*, p. 68, Abridged.)

Ultimately, when all that lives has reached the silence of Nirvana, desire itself in every form will die. Meanwhile this *Tanha*, and especially that aspect of it known as *kama*, called by Mrs. Rhys Davids "natural, unregenerate desire," must be sublimated into higher forms, giving way to aspirations and ideals for which a better term would be goodwill rather than good desire. To talk of killing all desire is foolish, for it is through purer forms of willing or desire that the lower inclinations are gradually transformed into altruistic aims.

Q.—What, then, do you mean by right desire?

A.—To one who really understands the Three Signs of Being, life can have no attraction. To such it is merely a school in which certain lessons must be learnt, in which the ignorance which binds us on the Wheel of Rebirth must be removed to leave us free to seek reunion with Reality. For such a man the objects of ambition such as wealth and fame, power and the plaudits of the multitude, make no appeal. He seeks enlightenment, and therefore scorns the perishable fruits of such desire, knowing full well, as Omar Khayyam knew, how

"The Worldly Hope men set their Hearts upon
Turns Ashes—or it prospers; and anon,
Like Snow upon the Desert's dusty Face
Lighting a little hour or two—is gone."

Nor does he crave for the gratification of the senses, for he knows that such can yield but a selfish, fleeting form of pleasure, which, by virtue of its perishable nature, ultimately reappears as pain. His position is, therefore, that of agreeing with Christ when he advised (Matthew 6, 19): "Lay not up for yourselves treasure upon earth, where moth and rust doth corrupt, and where thieves break through and steal," for as the Buddha proclaimed five hundred years before: "The real treasure is that laid up through charity and compassion, temperance and self-control. This treasure passes not away." (*Nidhikanda Sutta.*) A Buddhist's every act is based upon his knowledge of Life's unity. Therefore he knows that such desires as come from the separated self, those promptings of the passions which delude the mind into thinking "I want this and that," are contrary to the law of man's being. It follows that their gratification, certainly to the extent that it is obtained at the expense of others, or leads to lack of self-control, can only end in suffering. He therefore strives to eliminate desire for self, by gradually transmuting it into the higher channels of altruistic ideals. This alone is right desire, a powerful never-ceasing will-to-help, a constant striving towards the enlightening of mankind, based on the realisation of all that the simple phrase "the Unity of Life" implies. As is said in "Light on the Path": "When a man is able to regard his life as part of a whole, he will no longer struggle to obtain anything for himself," but will follow the immemorial law therein set out: "Desire to sow no seeds for your own harvesting; desire only to sow that seed, the fruit of which shall feed the world." Moreover, it is a fact which all will verify who have dedicated their lives to the service of humanity, that selfless desire carries with it the power to fulfil.

Q.—Why is that?

A.—Presumably because that which is in accordance with the Dhamma, regarded as the moral aspect of the Universal Law, will move towards its appointed end with all the vast momentum of that Law, while every desire that includes the thought of self must gain fulfilment in defiance of that Law. Therefore the teaching stands: "Desire nothing save the Good, the Beautiful, the True, and the welfare of mankind."

Q.—I understand that the Third Noble Truth simply states that the elimination of desire will remove the cause of man-made suffering.

A.—Of *all* suffering, for *Tanha* is the force that keeps us in the realms of Samsara, over which alone Dukkha holds sway. "The world is carried away by the stream of craving; from its whirlpool there is no salvation. But wisdom is a staunch vessel and meditation a firm support." (*Fo-sho-hing-tsang-ching*.) If there were no way out of this whirlpool of desire, Buddhism would indeed be a doctrine of despair. As is said in *The Light of Asia*:—

"If ye lay bound upon the wheel of change,
And no way were of breaking from the chain,
The Heart of Boundless Being is a curse,
The Soul of Things fell Pain.
Ye are not bound!"

for one description of Nirvana is the dying out of the three fires of *Lobha, Dosa* and *Moha;* Desire, Hatred and Illusion. "What is the root of evil? Craving, hatred and delusion are the root of evil. And what is the root of good? To be free from hatred, craving and delusion is the root of good." (*Samyutta Nikaya.*) From the quenching of these three fires comes Peace.

As *The Light of Asia* again says:

"The Third is Sorrow's Ceasing. This is Peace
To conquer love of self and lust of life,
To tear deep-rooted passion from the breast,
To still the inward strife;
For love to clasp Eternal Beauty close;
For glory to be Lord of self. . . ."

It is a peace that comes from a realisation of the universal point of view, the comprehensive vision of one who stands above all sects and creeds and narrow dogmatism, and sees all living things in one great forward movement from Samsara to Nirvana. Speaking of this Third Truth, Mr. Kingsland says, it is "to learn the truth of the larger life, which can be ours when we have put aside all strife for personal gratification and perceived the deeper current of spiritual life which flows from age to age, and abides for ever." (Esoteric Basis of Christianity, p. 18). He then goes on to say: "*When* these (Four Truths) have been learnt, we may place our feet on that Path at the end of which we may obtain liberation from birth and rebirth under Karmic Law, for we shall ourselves have become one with that law."

The Noble Eightfold Path.

Q.—Is this the Noble Eightfold Path, the existence of which is the Fourth Noble Truth?

A.—It is. But as Mr. Kingsland points out, it is only when we have grasped at least the first of the Truths that we can understand the significance of the fourth. As is said in *Light on the Path*: "No man desires to see that light which illumines the spaceless soul until pain and sorrow and despair have driven him away from the life of ordinary humanity." (p. 36.)

Those who appreciate this truth from their earliest years have realised it in some previous life.

This Noble Eightfold Path is the same Way that is found in all philosophies and faiths which claim to offer liberation from life's sufferings. As the Bhikkhu Silacara says (*Lotus Blossoms*, page 19): "The man who obeys the behests of morality, to whatever form of faith he belongs, is on the Path, whether he himself is aware of it or not. To that extent at least he may be called a Buddhist, for Buddhism is no mere creed. It is the Dhamma—the expression of the Law of all the worlds—the statement of the Norm of all Existence, high and low; other than in compliance wherewith is felicity for none." And H. P. Blavatsky, on the same theme, said, "Whatever differences are to be found in the various presentations of the Esoteric Doctrine . . . in every one of them we find the fullest agreement upon one point—the road to spiritual development. . . . Search as we may through the Bibles of every race and cult, we find but one way—hard, painful, troublesome—by which man can gain the true spiritual insight." (Adyar Pamphlets No. 71.) Viewed in the restricted sense of a moral code, it is the Path of strict morality taught by Confucius and Zoroaster; it is the Way of Taoism and the teaching of the Upanishads; it is the clear commandment of Christ which Europe never heard. It is neither the "habitual practice of sensuality; a low, unworthy way, nor the habitual practice of asceticism. There is a middle path O Bhikkhus, avoiding these two extremes—a Path which bestows understanding, which leads to peace of mind, to the higher wisdom, to Nirvana. It is Right Views or Knowledge, Right Aims or Motives, Right Speech and Right Conduct, Right Means of Livelihood, Right Effort, Right Mind-Control and Right Meditation," or spiritual union with Reality. (*Buddhist Suttas*, pp. 146-8.)

It is the Middle Way between the pairs of opposites, and leads in time to an understanding of such paradoxes as the simultaneous belief in the being and the non-being of the world. "That all is existent is one extreme; that all is non-existent is another extreme. The Tathagata, avoiding the two extremes, preaches his truth, which is the Middle Way." (*Vinaya* and *Samyutta Nikaya*.) But, as the Bhikkhu Silaĉara again points out (*Lotus Blossoms*) the Path is but a method or process for eliminating the cause of suffering—desire. It is a means and never an end. " Buddhism is a method and only a method, by which pain is banished and salvation from sorrow secured. . . . The method is a method of salvation by Enlightenment, not by emotion, and its three stages are: first, Morality, second, Mind-culture, and third, Wisdom." The Path may be regarded from the positive or negative point of view. Negatively it brings about dispassion by the slow elimination of the thirst for sensuous pleasure; positively it leads to pure compassion by the cultivation of a selfless love for all that lives. In the combination of the two lies liberation from the Wheel. From the mystic's point of view, each pilgrim must become the Way. As is said in the " Voice of the Silence," " Thou canst not travel on the Path before thou hast become that Path itself." Nor is this aspect found only in Buddhist works. " When this Path is beheld, whether one sets out to the East or to the West, to whatever place one would go, that place one's own self becomes." So said Krishna; and is not Christ reported to have said, " I am the Way, the Truth and the Life "? From yet another point of view the Path is that which leads from selfishness to altruism, from the unreal to the Real. It is the Path of Purity that all in time must tread, for though its forms be many there is but one Path. The word is, however, used in many senses. Strictly speaking only those are truly " treading the Path " who have put aside all worldly interests and have definitely " entered the stream." Such are Initiates of the Buddha-Wisdom itself. Of these we will speak later, but in the ordinary sense of the term all those are

"Pilgrims of the Middle Way" who, weary of this "fretful fever" life, have seriously set their faces away from its illusions towards the freedom and the silence of Nirvana. But though many profess to be striving for this great ideal, there are few whose will is strong enough to overcome the binding force of worldly interest and personal desires, for "one is the road that leads to wealth, another the road that leads to Nirvana." (**Dhammapada**, v. 75.)

Wherefore is Christ reported to have said, "Strait is the gate and narrow is the way . . . and few there be that find it." In a world in which the eyes of most men are blinded by ignorance and selfish desire, he who strives to win to self-perfection is indeed a pioneer, but to the extent that he succeeds he is an inspiration and example to his fellow-men. In the words of William James: "If things are ever to move upward, someone must be ready to take the first step. . . . No one who is not willing to try charity and non-resistance, as the saint is always willing, can tell whether these methods will or will not succeed." He then points out that when they do succeed, the power they wield for good is far superior to force or "worldly prudence," and concludes: "This practical proof that 'worldly wisdom' may be safely transcended is the saint's magic gift to mankind." (**Varieties of Religious Experience**, p. 358.)

Q.—Is the purpose of treading the Path only the liberation of the individual from suffering?

A.—We will discuss this under the comparative aims and objects of the two great schools, but for the moment we will say that in striving for liberation the Buddhist is but following the personal example of the All-Compassionate One, who sought for wisdom that each living thing might in the end be free. In setting out to find deliverance his motive was, as rendered in the *Light of Asia*:

"This will I do who have a realm to lose,
Because I love my realm, because my heart
Beats with each throb of all the hearts that ache,
Known and unknown, these that are mine and those
Which shall be mine, a thousand million more
Saved by this sacrifice I offer now."

Self-Reliance.

Q.—You have said that each must tread this Path alone. Can we not help each other?

A.—All may help each other, and should, but ultimately each must stand alone. The Buddhist attitude is summed up in one of the most famous of the Scriptures, the ***Maha-Parinibbana-Sutta*** (S.B.E. ed., p. 38): "Therefore, O Ananda, be ye lamps unto yourselves. Be ye a refuge to yourselves. Betake yourselves to no external refuge. Hold fast as a refuge to the truth. Look not for refuge to anyone besides yourselves. Work out your own salvation with diligence."

No teacher has ever given a more definite pronouncement on the necessity of self-reliance than is contained in these words.

Q.—But you agree that we may help one another on the Path?

A.—It is our duty to do so, for such is but the

practical application of the Buddhist belief in Brotherhood. As the Buddha said:

"A man that stands alone, having decided to obey the Dhamma, may be weak, and slip back into his old ways. Therefore, stand ye together, assist one another, and strengthen one another's efforts. Be like unto brothers; one in love, one in holiness, one in your zeal for the truth."

But though all life is one, the sober fact remains that in spite of the helping hands of friends; in spite of saints and sages pointing out the pitfalls on the Path that they themselves still tread, each unit of the one evolving life must ultimately tread the selfsame Path alone. Says the *Voice of the Silence* to the lonely neophyte: Prepare thyself, for thou wilt have to travel on alone. The teacher can but point the way." Throughout the ages men have sought for some vicarious method of salvation from their own shortcomings and misdeeds, whether by cruel sacrifice, or ardent prayer, or by the invention of an all-powerful God who could divert at will the course of cause and effect. But "be not deceived; God is not mocked; for whatsoever a man soweth, that shall he also reap." So said St. Paul, thus once more setting forth the Law of Karma to those who had ears to hear. In the words of the *Dhammapada* (v. 160/165): "By oneself the evil is done, by oneself one suffers; by oneself evil is left undone, by oneself one is purified. The pure and the impure stand or fall by themselves, for none can purify another."

Q.—Then there is no way in which the consequences of the acts of one man may be borne by another?

A.—As we shall see when we discuss Karma, the unity of Life involves the unity of Karma. The act of one becomes the act of all, whether its effects be good or bad. As Ananda Coomaraswamy says: "No man lives to himself alone, but we may regard the whole creation as one life, and therefore as sharing a common karma to which every individual contributes for good or ill." (*Buddha and the Gospel of Buddhism*, p. 231.)

From one point of view, therefore, the results of the acts of one man *are* borne, not by any one other, but by all. To this extent the power of compassion and goodwill may have the effect, by lessening the burden of the common karma of the world, of mitigating to a slight extent the suffering of others caused by violation of the Universal Law; but even if the greatest of the sons of men could bear the burden of another in a more direct degree than this, he would serve that other ill, for ultimately each must learn the lessons which suffering alone can teach. Would a child learn that fire is dangerous if *you* suffered pain when *it* put its fingers in the fire? The most a man can do, or should desire to do, to help his brother is to use the mighty power of compassion to enable him more easily to bear his burden, and to learn the lessons which his suffering alone can make him understand. Therefore the principle remains that both in sorrow and in joy, in triumph or the hour of need, each man must ultimately stand or fall by that strength and wisdom which the mystics, saints and sages of the past have ever testified comes only from within.

Q. But when you speak of "self"-reliance, what is the "self" on which you rely?

A. Let us briefly consider man as he is somewhat loosely analysed in the Buddhist Scriptures, and so, by process of elimination, find an answer to your question.

SECTION FOUR.

Self, Karma and Rebirth.

The Skandhas.

In the Buddhist Scriptures, then, man is described as being composed of five " groups " of qualities or attributes, called " *skandhas*." These groups of qualities are variously translated and described, but here we have adopted the minimum upon which all appear to be agreed. They may be considered as aspects or expressions of man's consciousness. The first is *Rupa*, form or body; in this sense, the physical body as including the organs of sense. It is the bundle of material qualities, properties or attributes. The second is *Vedana*, which includes the feelings or sensations, whether pleasant, unpleasant or neutral. The third is *Sañña*, comprising all perception or recognition, whether sensuous or mental. It is reaction to sense stimuli, described as " awareness with recognition," or the idea which arises from such reaction.

The fourth bundle, the *Sankharas*, includes all tendencies, mental and physical, the elements or factors in consciousness, the mental processes of discrimination and comparison between the ideas so brought into being.

Of all these bundles of attributes, so classified according to the function each performs, we can unhesitatingly say that this is not the Self we seek, for it is changing every moment, and having come into being must ultimately be dissolved. "Impermanent are *all* component things."

The fifth of the *Skandhas*, *Viññana*, is as perishable and fleeting as the others, but in its nature it presents more difficulty. It is variously translated as consciousness, mind, and mental powers, including the "mental, moral and physical predispositions." It is the equivalent of the "Higher Manas" of the *Secret Doctrine*, and of the Christian "soul" as understood by St. Paul. It is never the same for two moments together, being in a constant state of flux. It is the centre of conscious existence in its ever-changing forms, and as such, is as Mr. S. Z. Aung points out, "like the current of a river, which still maintains one constant form, one seeming identity, though not one single drop remains to-day of all the volume which composed that river yesterday." (Intro. to *Compendium of Philosophy*, p. 8.)

In this connection the word has a different meaning from "*Viññana*" as a link in the Chain of Causation or "Twelve Nidanas," as we shall see later. As one of the *skandhas* it appears to be equivalent to self-consciousness, the perception by the individual that he is at the moment different from his neighbour, the belief that "I am I and not you." This, as we shall see, is one of the "Fetters" that have to be broken before the aspirant attains Nirvana, and is known as *Sakkayaditthi*, the heresy of separateness, that is, of separate individual existence, the belief that the separated "personality" is the real man. But though this state of *Viññana* is necessarily impermanent, it is, during the long pilgrimage towards perfection, a fact which must be recognised. To this extent alone it may be treated as the soul of man, always remembering that it is impermanent and changing every moment of the day. "It is an aggregate of inconceivable complexity, the concentrated sum of the creative thinking of previous lives beyond all reckoning. It is the descendant of the forces generated in the past, a composite of millions of existences . . . From life to life these elements never combine in exactly the same way . . . Its force is cumulative; it becomes deepened and enriched with each successive experience." (*From a Lecture. Anon.*)

All consciousness is thus a constant flow, and "individual consciousness is the adaptation to specific purposes, by the body as an organ of action; of the flow of the universal consciousness." (Charlotte Woods epitomising Bergson in *The Self and its Problems*, *p.* 63.). The same writer (ibid p. 61) describing Wm. James' Transmission Theory, speaks of his belief in a "universally diffused eternal World-Soul whose pure white radiance is broken by the prism of the human body into the differentiated entities we call men," thus echoing Shelley in *Adonais*:

"The One remains, the many change and pass;
Heaven's light forever shines, Earth's shadows fly;
Life, like a dome of many-coloured glass,
Stains the white radiance of Eternity,
Until Death tramples it to fragments . . ."

This we believe to be a Western presentation of the Buddhist point of view.

Q. Then it is not on *Viññana* that we can rely?

A. Clearly not, for, as Bradley says (*Appearance and Reality*, p. 307). "The body and soul are phenomenal arrangements, which take their proper place in the constructed series of events, and in that character are both alike defensible and necessary. But neither is real in the end, each is merely phenomenal, and one has no title to fact which is not owned by the other," the soul or mind in fact, is mortal even as the outward body of clay.

The Will.

Q. What then remains? What of the human will?

A. The Will, or volition, is usually given as one of the *Sankharas*, or factors of consciousness. This is apparently because, while functioning on all planes, it is most noticeable as a quality of the mind, and this close relationship, bringing about the dynamic power of thought, is well expressed in the opening words of the *Dhammapada*, where we read: "All that we are is the result of what we have thought: it is founded on our thoughts, it is made up of our thoughts." Will is, therefore, the chief element in the bundle of *Sankharas*, and is, in fact, "the most dominant aspect of consciousness, the basal element of human life." (Radhakrishnan, *Indian Philosophy*, Vol. I., p. 404, where this complicated subject is discussed in its relation to other terms in Buddhist psychology.) Will, however, as with all else in the Universe, is sevenfold in outward form, and may appear as abstract energy or animal desire according to the plane or level of consciousness on which it is made manifest.

It is in itself an abstract and impersonal force, and as such is neither good nor bad. In the metaphysics of the Mahayana it is *Fohat*, that which binds together the two poles of Reality, Spirit and Matter, making with them a Cosmic Trinity which is the basis of all Trinities in every school of thought. But as *Fohat* is the same as *Mahat*, the Cosmic principle which manifests as Mind, we can see why the Buddhist places Will among the *Sankharas* or qualities of mind.

Will, then, is the driving force or energy which in a thousand forms controls the Universe, and gives the semblance of perpetual motion or becoming to that which always is about to be but never is. As such, it clearly cannot be regarded as the Self.

Q. But he who strengthens and develops his will is more self-reliant than his weak-willed neighbour?

A. Undoubtedly. Will being a universal force, exclusively possessed by none, "my will" and "your will" are strong or weak to the extent that each reflects, embodies or acts in harmony with the Cosmic Will. There is but one Will, or Universal Force, and he who cultivates the faculty of rightly directed Effort learns to draw increasingly upon that boundless store. But will is colourless. It is the motive with which it is used which makes it good or bad. As Terence says: "Things are according to the mind of him who possesses them. To him who knows how to use them they are good; to him who does not use them aright they are ill;" and as Shakespeare's *Hamlet* says: "There is nothing either good or bad but thinking makes it so." Strength of will is but a potent instrument to be used for good or evil at its user's choice. To the extent that he dedicates "his" will to purposes in harmony with the Universal Law, will he find his power for good increasing day by day, but if he strives to turn "his" will against the whole, he will meet with ever greater suffering, until, like a swimmer worn out with his efforts to overcome the current, he decides to swim downstream.

Q. Then what remains besides the *Skandhas* and the Will?

A. That is the question which we ask the Christian dogmatist. Where is there any room in man as he is cognisable to our intelligence, for any principle or faculty which is other than impermanent and, therefore, subject to decay? If then, there is a Self, it must be abstract and impersonal, unchanging and eternal, utterly beyond the senses and the analytic faculties of mind. The Self is, therefore, nothing less than that Ultimate Reality of which each human being sooner or later comes to feel the need, but which none can prove to another to be true. This only is the Self on which we may rely in fullest confidence; the exclusive property of no man yet the heart of all. It is, of course, no God, no person to be worshipped, but a Cosmic Principle, at once the Goal of mysticism and the source of all. It dwells in every man, yet none may call it his. Its vehicle is *Buddhi*, or *Bodhi*, the faculty of intuition, which, though latent as a higher aspect of the mind, has yet to be developed by the average man in the later stages of the Noble Eightfold Path. Ultimately all will use it for contacting this Reality in fullest consciousness, but this *Samadhi*, as the state of consciousness is called, is on the threshold of Nirvana, therefore for the vast majority of men a promise for the future rather than a faculty for present use. Whether or not, however, any man can at the moment realise the Self, at least its outward semblance is for all to see. Each varied form from mineral to man is but a fragmentary expression of this Self, and by its power slowly "moves to righteousness," to ultimate reunion with the source from which it came. It is of the realisation of this Unity that Krishna speaks in the great Hindu epic, the *Bhagavad-Gita*, when he describes true knowledge as distinct from false. We quote from Sir Edwin Arnold's poetic version, *The Song Celestial* (p. 103):

> "There is true knowledge. Learn thou it in this:
> To see one changeless Life in all the Lives,
> And in the separate, One Inseparable.
> There is imperfect knowledge: that which sees
> The separate existences apart,
> And, being separated, holds them real . . ."

From this concept we get the great antithesis, the false self and the true. The false self is the egoistic self, the fleeting personality, the actor's mask through which the true man speaks. The true Self is One, being an aspect of the Universal Law; the Not-Self in its myriad forms, the countless units of evolving life, opposes, owing to the personal desires which spring from ignorance, the mighty purpose of the Whole. From this in turn comes friction, *Dukkha*, only to be removed by transmutation of these personal desires from selfish, separative ends, to those in harmony with all.

Q. Then Self-Reliance means reliance on the Buddhist equivalent of God?

A. You may put it that way if you please, so long as you remember that it is the "God within." It is the One Unknowable, no person but a Universal Law, which men have variously described as Wisdom, Beauty, Love, Truth, the Dhamma, and a thousand other names for That which is unnameable.

Q. Then the Universe as we know it is unreal, the Not-Self, an illusion?

A. That is so, for nothing in the Universe is constant for one moment; all is in a process of becoming; nothing *is*. "Coming to be, coming to be; ceasing to be, ceasing to be." So the Buddha summed up all existence.

The Wheel of Causation.

Q. Presumably there is some Law inherent in this seeming chaos?

A. The basis of existence is, in Buddhist teaching, an intricate net-work of causation, or, more accurately, interrelation of events and actions on all planes. This vast conception is presented in the symbol of an ever-turning wheel, the Wheel of Life, *Samsara*, having twelve spokes, the Twelve Nidanas or component factors in its ceaseless turning. The subject of Causation is, however, far too deep to be considered fully here. The Buddha himself described it as profound, not easily to be completely understood, and H. P. Blavatsky, having touched upon the Twelve Nidanas in her *Glossary*, remarks (p. 213):

" Belonging to the most subtle and abstruse doctrines of the Eastern metaphysical system, it is impossible to go into the subject at any greater length."

The spokes are usually enumerated as follows: Old Age and Death and all the suffering which life entails are caused by *Jati*—Birth. The cause of *Jati* is Becoming, coming into being, *Bhava*, which is the karmic agent of rebirth, as caused in turn by powerful Attachment or *Upadana*, which is the craving for and clinging to life. " It typifies attachment to worldly things which the human being ignorantly grasps at, supposing they will quench this craving thirst which has arisen from sensation." (*Buddhism* (Lectures) Rhys Davids, p. 159, Putnam.) The cause of this attachment, then, is craving, *Tanha*, or desire for sentient existence,

" That thirst which makes the living drink
Deeper and deeper of the salt sea waves
Whereon they float—pleasures, ambition, wealth,
Praise, fame or domination, conquest, love;
Rich meats and robes, and fair abodes and pride
Of ancient lines, and lust of days, and strife
To live, and sins that flow from strife . . ."

So says the *Light of Asia*, yet desire is brought about by *Vedana* or Feelings. This perception by the senses is in turn produced by *Phassa*, Contact, the connecting link between the organs of sense and the objects they cognise, while the organs of sense, six in number, are produced by *Nama-Rupa*, literally Name and Form. The Organs of Sense are the usual five, with the addition of the mind. Nama-Rupa is more difficult. It is the Form and its significance, or, conversely, the meaning and the form through which it is expressed. But although a self-contained conception it is usually considered in conjunction with its cause *Viññana*, Consciousness in general, which to become self-conscious needs a form or vehicle through which to gain experience and be "itself." Even as a river is only such by virtue of the limitations of its banks, else would it be but a nameless undivided portion of the sea, so must this abstract consciousness submit to limitation in order that it may express itself in terms of time and space. This Nama-Rupa, then, becomes equivalent to personality, a symbol of the necessary "body of illusion" which the abstract must indue before it can appear in concrete form. It therefore is the birth of egoism, of the sense of separateness possessed by each fragment of reality which imagines that *its* "self" is separate from the Universal Self from which it came. *Nama Rupa* and *Viññana*, therefore, are more closely interdependent than any others of the endless chain, for whereas Name and Form imply the life which they express, the consciousness within could never be made manifest without its vehicle or form.

Viññana, of course, has many forms. We have seen how it precipitates *Nama-Rupa* in the same way as thought precipitates action on the physical plane, but *Viññana* is in turn the outcome of the *Sankharas*, here equivalent to Karma in the sense of action in the three worlds of illusion, the mental, emotional and physical planes. But Karma. in this sense, is in turn the child of Ignorance, *Avidya*, which is the father of all human suffering, and the basis of causation regarded from whatever point of view.

Such are the Twelve *Nidanas* which Dr. Paul Carus has helpfully though loosely paraphrased in the following way (*Gospel of Buddha*, p. 40): "In the beginning there is existence blind and without knowledge; and in this sea of ignorance there are stirrings formative and organising. From this there arises awareness . . . which . . . . begets organisms that live as individual beings. These develop the six fields, that is, the five senses and the mind. The six fields come in contact with things. Contact begets sensation which creates the thirst of individualised being. This creates a cleaving to things which produces the growth and continuation of selfhood. Selfhood continues in renewed births. These renewed births of selfhood are the cause of suffering, old age, sickness and death. They produce lamentation, anxiety and despair."

In the *Samyutta Nikaya* we have the twelve links analysed in terms of time. Ignorance causes actions which in turn produce fresh moments of awareness or percipient consciousness. So much for the Past, but these produce the necessity for another life on earth, the Present, when *Nama Rupa*, product of *Viññana*, causes sense organs to appear which lead to contact, then to feeling, craving and grasping. So much for the Present, but this grasping, *Tanha*, causes a fresh life in the Future, from which rebirth come suffering, disease, old age and death. "*That* being present, *this* becomes; *this* being present, *that* becomes . . . Such is the coming to pass of this entire mass of suffering."

The basic root is sometimes given as Avidya, Ignorance, but sometimes as Desire. Both may be used according to the type of mind and the point of view from which the Wheel is regarded, as is well explained in Warren's *Buddhism in Translations* at page 175, but desire itself is caused by ignorance, and hence to this extent, the two are one.

Thus, like the revolutions of a wheel, there is a regular succession of death and birth, the moral cause of which is the cleaving to existing objects, while the instrumental cause is Karma.

To stop the turning of the wheel, we must therefore remove its moral cause, desire, or cleaving to illusion. From this point of view, as Professor Rhys Davids pointed out, the doctrine of causation " with its positive formula of uprising and its negative formula of passing away, covers the ground of the second and third of the (Four Noble) Truths." (*Dialogues of the Buddha*, Part 2, p. 44.)

It must be noted that the " spokes " of the wheel are not to be considered only in the order given; still less are they necessarily sequential in time. They are rather the interrelated factors in an endless whole. As Professor Anesaki says in his brilliant Appendix on Reality in " Nichiren the Buddhist Prophet " at page 154, "The Buddhist conception of causation is applied to any relation of interaction, interdependence, correlation or co-ordination, founded on an intrinsic necessity. . . . The Buddhist would not confine the *causal* relation within the idea of *time* relation."

Note the dual aspect of the Wheel from the viewpoint of the purpose for which its existence was taught. It is at once a way of explaining phenomena in general, and *Dukkha* in particular, and in its reversed form the method by which the causes of *Dukkha* may be destroyed.

The law of causation is co-extensive with the Universe in place, time and subject. With regard to this last "dimension" of causation Dr. McGovern says: "Buddhism distinguishes itself from other systems by applying the doctrine of causality and non-substantiality to the mind as well as to the body." (*Manual of Buddhist Philosophy*, Vol. I., page 167.) Even the Buddhas cannot change the operation of this Law. They can but show a Way which leads to a state of consciousness beyond its power, the spiritual counterpart of the centre of the hub, where in the midst of motion there is peace.

Evolution.

Q. But is there no purpose behind this ceaseless movement?

A. Buddhism accepts the principle of evolution, as against that of creation, and the existence of a plan or ordered purpose behind its operation, without examining in any detail what this vague conception means. Evolution is an interconnected growth of the life and the form.

In the latter, slowly growing as it does from mineral to vegetable, through vegetable to animal, and so in time to man, the Buddhist takes comparatively little interest, seeing that it is but a consideration of the "fetters of illusion" from which he struggles to be free. With the indwelling life, however, he has all to do, for he is ever striving towards that state of consciousness, Nirvana, when the Spirit or the Life within will have reached complete emancipation from matter in all its forms. Therefore he concentrates his attention on the treading of the Path which leads thereto, and leaves to those who think it worth their while the task of analysing how this matter is itself evolving, or, shall we say, *in*volving downwards before, on the returning arc, it enters on its *ev*olution back to the perfection whence it came.

"All trees and grass, these also shall in time be Buddha," says a Japanese proverb, "Buddha" meaning here, we think, "enlightened," even as Gautama was called the Buddha, the Enlightened One.

For further description of this cyclic motion of the Universe, this forward motion from illusion to enlightenment, we can but quote from the Eighth Book of the *Light of Asia*, where the author says:—

"Before beginning and without an end,
  As space eternal and as surety sure,
Is fixed a Power divine which moves to good.
  Only its laws endure.

. . . .

It will not be contemned of any one;
  Who thwarts it loses, and who serves it gains;
The hidden good it pays with peace and bliss,
  The hidden ill with pains.

. . . . . .

Such is the Law which moves to righteousness,
  Which none at last can turn aside or stay;
The heart of it is Love, the end of it
  Is peace and consummation sweet. Obey!"

But this world-order is a moral one. The converse is unthinkable. On man's intuitive belief that all existence is, however slowly, and by whatever devious ways, moving towards the Ideal, is based his ethics, culture, and moral codes, and all the spiritual greatness which his finest representatives have shown forth in the past.

The trend of science and the dogmas of religion in the West agree that evolution tends to a definite and a moral end, while differing as yet upon the nature of that end. Indeed, one of our leading philosophic writers, William James, has said of religion itself, as apart from any of its countless forms, that it consists in "the belief that there is an unseen order, and that our supreme good lies in harmoniously adjusting ourselves thereto," (*Varieties of Religious Experience*, p. 58) while in a later chapter (*ibid*, p. 101) he quotes that leader of "New Thought," Ralph Waldo Trine, as saying, "To recognise our own divinity, and our intimate relation to the Universal, is to attach the belts of our machinery to the power-house of the Universe. . . . We can rise to any heaven we ourselves choose; and when we choose to rise, all the highest powers of the

Universe combine to help us heavenward." (From *In Tune with the Infinite.*)

Nor are the poets silent on man's destiny.

As is said in "The Conversion of the King" (p. 21):

"No God of Fortune, neither Luck nor Chance
Decrees the narrow circle of our days.
The eyes of evolution are not blind.
There is a Plan, a vast and noble Plan
Behind the seeming chaos of our lives.
The rise and fall of Empire, birth and death,
And every little happening that seems
Of nothing worth, acts but a chosen part
Within the mighty drama of that Plan.
All is a slow becoming. Nothing is.
No living thing but moves with silent feet
Slowly towards its pre-appointed end,"

which is that "one far-off divine event to which the whole creation moves," which men have called by many names, but the Buddhists by the name Nirvana. Of this we will speak later.

Karma, or Cause and Effect.

Q. Tell me more of this "Law which moves to righteousness."

A. It is called in Sanskrit, *Karma*, and in Pali, *Kamma*, that is, simply "action," "doing," "deed." It may be considered as Cause, Effect, and the Law which regulates the perfect equilibrium of the two. For two thousand years have Christians heard it proclaimed from their pulpits, yet having ears to hear they heard not, neither did they understand. "Be not deceived," say the Scriptures; "God is not mocked, for whatsoever a man soweth, that shall he also reap," and is not the Christ reported to have said upon the Mount: "Judge not that ye be not judged, for with what judgment ye judge ye shall be judged, and with what measure ye mete, it shall be measured to you again."

From the Buddhist viewpoint, Karma is the converse of the Christian presentation of this Law. Whatsoever a man doth reap, say the Buddhists, that has he also sown. Believing in the operation of unswerving natural justice, Buddhism would say in reply to the Biblical enquiry: "Who did sin, this man or his parents, that he was born blind?" that it was *this man* who had sinned, that is, had so behaved in a previous life as to cause in the life in question the effect of blindness. As Mrs. Rhys Davids says in "*Buddhism*" at page 124, "Afflictions are for Buddhists so many forms, not of pre-payment by which future compensation may be claimed, but of settlement of outstanding debts accruing from bad, that is to say from evil-bringing, unhappiness-promoting acts, done either in this life or in previous lives." In Karma only is to be found, in conjunction with its commonsense corollary, Rebirth, a perfect, natural and therefore reasonable answer to the apparent injustice of the daily round. Why should this man be born a beggar, this a prince? Why this a cripple with a twisted blackened heart, this a genius, that a fool? Why this a high-born Indian woman, that a low-born English man? These are effects. Do the causes lie in the hands of an irresponsible and finite God, or, as the Buddhists say, within the lap of Law?

"We are familiar," says Professor Rhys Davids, "with the doctrine of the indestructibility of force, and can therefore understand the Buddhist dogma that no exterior power can destroy the fruit of a man's deeds, that they must work out their full effect to the pleasant or the bitter end." (*Buddhism*, S.P.C.K. p. 103-4.) As it is man who suffers the effects, so it is man who generates the cause, and having done so cannot flee the consequences. Says the *Dhammapada* (165): "By oneself the evil is done; by oneself one suffers. By oneself evil is left undone; by oneself one is purified." And again in verse 127, "Not in the sky, not in the midst of the sea, nor anywhere else on earth is there a spot where a man may be freed from (the consequences of) an evil deed." Thus is every man the moulder of his "life to come" and master of his destiny.

> "Ye suffer from yourselves. None else compels.
> None other holds you that ye live and die,
> And whirl upon the Wheel, and hug and kiss
> Its spokes of agony . . . . . ."

So says the *Light of Asia*, and the West has voiced the self-same truth throughout the ages, for the thought was never new. "Subsequents follow antecedents by a bond of inner consequence; no merely numerical sequence of arbitrary and isolated units, but a rational interconnection." So said the Emperor Marcus Aurelius, and speaking of the abstract laws of the Universe, Emerson said they "execute themselves . . . . In the soul of man there is a justice whose retributions are instant and entire. He who does a good deed is instantly ennobled. He who does a mean deed is by the action itself contracted" (*Miscellanies*), and again: "Secret retributions are always restoring the level, when disturbed, of the divine justice. It is impossible to tilt the beam. Settles for evermore the ponderous equator to its line, and man and mote, and star and sun, must range to it, or be pulverised by the recoil." (*Lectures and Biographical Studies*.—EMERSON.)

The Western poets have frequently sensed the presence of this law, yet was it a woman, cradled in the Christian faith, who gave it best expression when she said:

"From body to body your spirit speeds on;
It seeks a new form when the old one has gone,
And the form that it finds is the fabric you wrought
On the loom of the mind with the fibre of thought.
As dew is drawn upwards, in rain to descend,
Your thoughts drift away and in destiny blend,
You cannot escape them, or petty or great,
Or evil or noble, they fashion your fate."

(*From "The Law," by Ella Wheeler Wilcox.*)

From this it will be noticed that it is the mind which moulds man's destiny, action being but precipitated thought. It follows that one's lightest thought has vast effects, not only on the thinker but on all that lives. Hence the tremendous power of hatred and of love, which man, in childlike ignorance, is indiscriminately pouring out upon the world by night and day. It needs but commonsense to see how such dynamic qualities, carefully controlled and cultivated, can ultimately make a man just what he wills to be. Karma is thus the very antithesis of fatalism. That which is done can by the doer be in time undone. That which is yet to be depends on the deeds now being done.

There is here no cruel Nemesis, only the slow and perfect action of an all-embracing Law.

The Buddhist would agree with Omar Khayyam when he wrote:

> "The Moving Finger writes; and having writ,
> Moves on: nor all thy Piety nor Wit
> Shall lure it back to cancel half a Line,
> Nor all thy Tears wash out a Word of it."

But though the record of a deed remains indelible, it is the sufferer whose finger wrote his destiny, and who had it in his power to choose whether the deed were good or bad. It is but just that he who disturbed should in the end restore the Universal equilibrium.

An individual's karma, in the sense of the sum of unexpended causes generated by him in the past, the burden which he has to bear upon life's pilgrimage, is classified with great precision in the various Eastern Schools, but can be analysed along the lines of Western Science by any student for himself. Karma is an ever-generating force. It may be as a thunder-cloud, so fully charged that nothing can delay its equally complete discharge. It may be as a snowball on the mountain side, so small and slowly moving that a slight expenditure of effort will suffice to overcome its motion, and so to bring its swiftly growing power to rest. Other analogies applicable to the handling of any natural force may be found with ease. Our object here is rather to explain its nature than to analyse its functioning.

The Buddhist, then, replaces Nemesis and Providence, Kismet, Destiny and Fate, with Universal, All-embracing Law, by his knowledge of which he moulds his future, hour by hour, a conception thus admirably summed up by a western student:

"Sow a thought, reap an act;
Sow an act, reap a habit;
Sow a habit, reap a character;
Sow a character, reap a destiny."

But even as the causes generated by one react upon that one, so the mass causation of a group, be it family, society or nation, reacts upon that group as such, and all whose karma placed them at the time therein. Each man has, therefore, many "karmas," racial, national, family, and personal, yet all quite properly *his*, else he would not have found himself subject to their sway.

An understanding of the law of Karma leads

to self-reliance, for in proportion as we understand its operation shall we cease to complain of our circumstances, and with the weakness of a child, turn to a man-made God to save us from the natural consequences of our acts. Karma is no God, for the Gods themselves are subject to its sway. "Only the ignorant personify Karma, and attempt to bribe, petition or cajole it; the enlightened know that they must understand it and conform to it" (From an anonymous pamphlet entitled "*An Introduction to the Essential Principles of the Dhamma*"). The wise man seeks for the causes of the effects he did not like, and either removes the cause or neutralises the effect by causes of a different kind.

The Universe itself is an effect; hence all the units in it, viewed as events, are at once both cause and effect within a vast Effect. Each is at once the result of all that has preceded it and the cause or partial cause of all to come. Yet, as we saw when studying Causation, Karma is not only cause and effect in time; rather is it the Law which governs the inter-relation and solidarity of the Universe in all its parts, and hence in a way, the karma of one such unit is the karma of all. Life being one, it is "the interdependence of Humanity which is the cause of what is called *Distributive Karma*, and it is this law which affords the solution to the great question of collective suffering and relief. No man can rise superior to his individual failings without lifting, be it ever so little, the whole body of which he is an integral part. In the same way no one can sin, nor suffer the effects of sin, alone." (*Key to Theosophy*, H. P. Blavatsky, p. 203.)

All action has its due result. A stone thrown into a pond causes wavelets to circle outwards to a distance proportionate to the initial disturbance; after which the initial state of equilibrium is restored. Such is the general law, but its application to the individual operates in the following way:

"Since each disturbance starts from some particular point it is clear that equilibrium and harmony can only be restored by the re-converging *to that same point* of all the forces which were set in motion from it." (*Ibid.* 206.)

Thus the consequences of an act re-act, via all the Universe, upon the doer, with a force commensurate with his own. Hence the futility of theories born of man's selfishness by which he imagines that some other breast than his own shall receive the pendulum's returning blow.

The Buddhist, then, by his understanding of the Law by which he lives, can wield it to a chosen noble end, and ever swimming with the current of his inmost being, reach in time "the other shore," Nirvana, the abode of Peace.

These principles, however, must be applied to be intelligible. Consider as an example the recent war. This was an effect, though, as a powerful cause, its own effects are with us still. It therefore had a cause commensurate with the force with which it burst forth in the world of men. Generally speaking, as we have seen, the cause of a physical event lies on the mental plane. Suppose, for example, it was hatred, slowly growing through the years between the European nations, hidden from the eye yet ever banking up, like thunder-clouds before the flash which bursts their pent-up energy and causes it to manifest as storm.

Such was, we think, the cause and such the terrible effect, but—and here is the lesson to be learnt—so long as equal causes slowly accumulate upon the plane of thought, so long will the like effects inevitably burst out in the world of men.

The limitations of space forbid us further to exemplify the application of this cosmic principle, but any thinking man and woman can watch the application of the law every moment of the day, and see, not only that it *is* the law, but that it is impersonal and absolutely just.

Q. You spoke of the effects in this life being the outcome of causes generated in a previous life. Have we then lived before?

Rebirth.

A. We have described rebirth as a corollary of Karma, and we adhere to that description. He who commits an act must sooner or later reap its consequences. Would it be just if by the way of suicide a man could finally end his life and so escape the consequences of a life of villainy?

Q. But could he not suffer in the world to come the effects of deeds committed in this?

A. The Buddhist answers "not completely." How can a physical cause fail to have a physical effect, whatever reflex action may be involved upon the mental or other planes? Cause and effect are equal and opposite. Now Karma involves the element of time: is it reasonable to say that all the causes generated in an average human life will produce their full effect before the last day of that period, and can the greatest of the lessons we are here to learn be mastered in that time? It is a quaint conceit to imagine so, for the oldest sages would admit that at the close of a life of study their wisdom is as a raindrop to the sea.

Q. This idea is new and foreign to the West.

A. It may appear so at the moment, but almost every country of the East accepts it as too obvious to need proof, and anthropologists have traced its presence in the legends and indigenous ideas of nearly every country in the world. It is to be found in most of the leading minds of Europe and America, from Plato to Origen, from Blake to Schopenhauer, from Goethe, Boehme, Kant and Swedenborg, to Browning, Emerson, Walt Whitman and the leading minds of the Western world to-day. For those who wish to realise how widespread is the doctrine in the West we recommend the study of E. D. Walker's *Reincarnation* (William Rider) in which the whole conception, with "authorities," is carefully set out. Here, however, we prefer to let the doctrine rest on its own inherent reasonableness, rather than to rely on the fact that so many others have accepted it as true. But for the Christian reader we would point out that it is clearly present in such mutilated fragments of Christ's teachings as are still extant. Consider, for example, the widely current rumours that he was John the Baptist, Jeremiah or Elijah come again (Matt. xvi, 13-16). Even Herod seemed to think that he was "John the Baptist risen from the dead" (*Mark* vi, 14-16). See also *Mark* ix, 11-13.

But the doctrine of rebirth was no more stressed by Christ than by the Buddha, for in each case those who listened had been born and bred in such belief, which formed a common background for the many sects and creeds in Palestine and India respectively.

Q. Nevertheless, the idea is revolutionary to the Christian mind. Can you prove it to be true?

A. Can anything worth knowing be completely proved? Is not the test to see whether it be reasonable? Consider the Buddhist teaching of an ever-growing something, called for the purpose of argument "soul," which moves from life to life, now clothed in a body of this sex, race and colour, class and creed, and now in one of that, gradually mastering the lessons it is here to learn until, in the round of time, the last of the fetters of illusion is removed and this "undivided portion of the Whole" enters that Nirvana to which it ever moves. Is not this concept far more reasonable, dignified and just than that which obtains among the spiritually youthful of the West, that of an immortal soul, precipitated by an unknown God into bestial or princely circumstances as His Will decides, halting upon the earth it may be but a few brief years, and then, at the "Day of Judgment," being judged according to the way in which it used its opportunities? Is not the former teaching more in accord with reason, logic and the voice of common-sense?

A life on earth is, to a Buddhist, as a wayside Inn upon a long white road. At any given moment there are many travellers therein, and even as we speak more enter through the doors of Birth, and others leave—by one whose name is Death. Within the common meeting-room are met together men of every type, whose intercourse with one another forms that reaction to environment we call experience.

Such an attitude to life enormously affects all blood relationship. The child may be an older pilgrim than its parents, and at the least, is quite entitled to its point of view. In the West we say that the child of a musical father is musical (if it be so) because of its heredity. In Buddhist lands it would be explained that the child was born into a musical family, because it (the child) had developed musical propensities in previous lives, and was attracted to an environment suitable for the expression of those propensities: a reversal of the Western view of cause and effect. The age of the body is thus no criterion of the age of the Pilgrim using it.

Q. I suppose rebirth explains the curious precocity of certain children?

A. How else can the scores of cases now on record be explained? "Infant prodigies" are but the normal outcome of a series of lives devoted to the evolution of a special faculty.

The latter is an effect whose cause can only be attributed to " freaks of nature," or the reasonable doctrine of rebirth.

Q. But the body at least is the product of its parents?

A. Certainly. So may a house be built by a landlord, but the tenant need not take it over as his residence against his will, but even though the body be not the direct creation of that " soul " which uses it, yet was it chosen as the instrument most suited to the needs of the informing life.

Q. This is all very strange to the Western mind.

A. Undoubtedly; and a whole volume would be needed to explain the subject from all its points of view. Our aim is merely to provide in Karma and Rebirth a double key to unexplained phenomena, and leave our readers to unlock such mysteries therewith as they desire. The idea of rebirth is not really difficult. Life does not die at the body's death, nor do the consequences of a deed. Forms are created and destroyed; they come into being, serve their purpose and then die, but the Life within knows no such limitation.

> " Nay, but as when one layeth
>   His worn-out robes away,
> And, taking new ones, sayeth,
>   ' These will I wear to-day '!
> So putteth by the spirit
>   Lightly its garb of flesh,
> And passeth to inherit
>   A residence afresh."

So said Sir Edwin Arnold in his verse translation of the great Hindu epic, the *Bhagavad-Gita*, and subject to a clear understanding of what it is that "passeth" on from life to life, the Buddhist would agree.

The Nature of Death.

Q. Death, then, is by no means final?

A. Certainly not. The body came into being: it must therefore one day die. Hence the Buddhist saying, "The cause of death is not disease, but birth." To mourn for the inevitable dissolution of a temporary garment is foolishness, all the more so when the man who has thus cast off his outer clothing will probably return to earth to meet again, maybe, the friends he knew before. Karma takes no reckoning of time. A bond of love or hate between two persons is a cause that will need those persons for the ultimate discharging of a like effect. Karma can wait, if need be, for ten thousand years. Death is usually nothing but a well-earned rest, when the experience, great or small, of one life is quietly digested, to appear in later lives as faculty, ability, and innate tendency. It is but an incident of life, and viewed from the standpoint of a thousand lives, an incident of as little importance and finality as sleep.

When Chuang Tzu wrote the following of his Master, Lao Tzu, the re-discoverer of Taoism, he might have been alluding to the Buddha's death: "When the Master came it was at the proper time; when he went away it was the simple sequence of his coming. Quiet acquiescence in what happens at its proper time, and quietly submitting to its ceasing, afford no occasion for grief or joy." What applies to a Buddha, who will come again no more, applies *a fortiori* to a humbler man.

Q. Then you agree with the Christian idea of death as the gateway to a fuller life?

A. To a different form of life, certainly, but strictly limited in duration by the thoughts and acts of the individual. How can the consequences of a finite life be infinite anything—Heaven or Hell? A man's hereafter is the aggregate effect of the causes generated by him on this earth. The cause was limited: equally so will be the effects. The limited and finite cannot cause eternity. Each man, the Buddha taught, suffers in after life the hell or heaven which he slowly manufactured every hour of his life on earth. The "Day of Judgment" is at all times and for everyone—To-day.

Q. You said that we sometimes meet our friends beyond the veil of death. When?

A. On our return to earth. The intervening worlds are entirely subjective, but if there is a strong link of love or hate between two persons they will, sooner or later, be brought together on earth to face the consequences, pleasant or unpleasant, of that link, by the patient and unswerving Law.

Q. But if we return to earth, why do we not remember our past lives?

A. Because physical memory needs a physical brain, and the brain which remembers incidents of this life is different from that which registered the deeds of the one before. But in fact the bridge from life to life can sometimes be, and has been, crossed. Students claim to have trained their memories to go back step by step, until in many cases they arrive at a clear and accurate memory of their previous life or lives. The subsequent verification of remembered scenery, surroundings and events, seems to prove the truth of the experimenter's claims. The Buddhist Scriptures abound in examples of this interesting but unprofitable exercise.

Q. But if the operator's brain is new in each life, how does the brain of this life remember the facts of the last?

A. Before we can answer this, we must consider what it is that is reborn.

This question is the subject of much futile argument, but the details are of no importance in the treading of the Eightfold Path. The body dies at death, but the individual's karma, the resultant of all the causes generated by him in the past, lives on. This complex "soul," the product of ten thousand lives, is clothed as we have seen, with divers attributes or qualities, cross-classified in early Buddhism as the *skandhas* other than the physical vehicle which dies at death. This it is, which in the intervening and subjective worlds which lie between two lives, digests the lessons of the previous life until such causes as can take effect subjectively have been transmuted into faculty and innate tendency. That which remains to incarnate afresh may be regarded as an individual, as in the Northern School of Buddhism, or as nameless complex residuum of karma, as in the Southern School. The danger of the former viewpoint lies in the tendency to look upon this individual as a "separated soul" eternally distinct from other forms of life. The Southern viewpoint, on the other hand, anxious to enforce the doctrine of *anatta* in its literal sense, keeps to the letter rather than the spirit of the Buddha's metaphors. One candle lighted from another—is the light of the second the same light as the first? Such imagery has its dangers to a certain type of mind, and leads in them to logical absurdity. Yet is the simile beautiful when understood. The Light, or Life, is One; the candles, fragments of its unity. Light one candle from another and the light is the same, yet different; the same in essence, yet seeming, maybe, to the outward eye to shine more brightly than before. Perhaps the wax which formed the second candle was more purified, the wick of finer texture and the whole created from a finer mould. To that extent the second differs from the first, yet the Light or Life was one and the same, more brightly shining in the second case because of the purer "skandhas" of its form. A volume might be written round this simple metaphor.

Between the disputing schools the "Middle Way" is surely to regard the man of one life as the karmic child of all his lives before, the product and creation of his own deliberate past. On the one hand man is "an undivided portion of a vast eternal Whole"; on the other hand the nameless, soulless, outcome of the action of his *skandhas* in the past.

Perhaps the distinction between the reincarnating *individual*, and the *personality* which lasts only one life, may help to make the doctrine clear. Everyone knows from experience this fundamental difference; the rebel self which seeks the gratification of its purely selfish desires, and the ruling or controlling self which, in the knowledge of the former's wrong-doing, strives to control it as a driver struggles to control a restive steed. Is not evolution a ceaseless warfare of the two, in which through many a bitter failure the individual learns to express himself through an ever more controlled and hence more perfect mask or personality? True, the Southern School has chosen rather to cling to the denial of the permanence of the personality than to consider the continuity and relative permanence of the karma-composed individual or transmigrating "soul." The distinction is, nevertheless, made clear by the late Col. Olcott in his *Buddhist Catechism* at page 52, where in a footnote he says: "The successive appearances on earth of the *skandhas* of a certain being are a succession of personalities. In each birth the *personality* differs from that of the previous, or next succeeding birth, but though personalities ever shift, the one long life along which they are strung like beads runs unbroken. It is, therefore, an individual vital undulation which careers through the objective side of nature under the impulse of Karma and the creative direction of Tanha. (Cannot we regard) the life-undulation as individuality and each of its natal manifestations as a separate personality? We *must* have two words to distinguish between the concepts . . . ." (Abridged.)

This distinction explains how it is but just that

Smith should in this life suffer the consequences of the misdeeds of one who in a past life was known as Brown. Though they are in one sense different men, yet fundamentally they are the same, even as an old man is different from, yet the same as, himself when young. For Smith of to-day is but the Brown of yesterday in a different suit of clothes. Whether we call what is reborn the resultant of all karma of the past, or a growing, changing individual, is only a matter of words; the doctrine is the same.

We can now answer your last question. The brain is of the one-life personality, while memory is an attribute of the *skandhas* or individuality which, ever-changing, passes on from life to life. Hence, while the brain remembers nothing earlier than its own "creation" at the body's birth, the essential man remembers all that ever happened to him in his previous lives. When the time comes in his evolution that his consciousness can function on the plane of pure mentality, unhindered by the blinding veils of flesh and other worldly "attributes," he will perceive all previous incarnations as a line of milestones on that "Road which leads from Suffering to Peace."

Q. But if life on earth is filled with Dukkha, why do we return?

A. Because, if the paradox be understood, we choose to do so against our will, that is, either deliberately or in ignorance we set in motion in one life causes which automatically bring us back for their fulfilment. We saw (page 54) how the cause of attachment to worldly things is *Tanha*, the cause of which in turn is pleasurable feelings caused by contact with the objects of sense. But pleasurable feelings beget the desire for their repetition. This desire, until sublimated or transmuted into worthier aspirations, acts as a powerful magnet between the Pilgrim and the world of sense, and though at death the worldly body dies, the craving or desire lives on. In the course of time this unappeased desire remodels from the unexhausted karma of the past a personality which, as a well-made suit of clothes, will perfectly express the individual who, in the interval between two lives, will in the ordinary way have benefited by his previous lives' experience, and be an "older," more mature and better man. It follows that until *Tanha* is completely sublimated into higher forms the man in question will continue to return, nor will its force be overcome until the last of the lessons he is here to learn is fully mastered, and the Eightfold Path of self-liberation has been trodden to the very end.

Q. Then sex is a matter of the physical body in which we happen to appear?

A. That is all, but "happen to appear" is not a matter of chance. The distinctive qualities of the sexes are complementary, and all must be made manifest in any individual before he or she can become a Master of the Wisdom, the "Man of Perfect Virtue" of the Chinese Sages, or, to the Buddhist mind, "a Perfectly Enlightened One."

SECTION FIVE.

The Noble Eightfold Path.

Q. Then to avoid rebirth we must kill out this craving for sensuous enjoyment by transmuting it into concentrated effort for the welfare of our fellow men?

A. That is so, and the way to that end was pointed out by the Buddha in the fourth of the Noble Truths, the Noble Eightfold Path. We have already briefly considered its nature at pages 61-4, and it will be seen that it contains little which is not found equally in other schools of thought. But the importance of Buddhist ethics lies not so much in their nature as in the great stress laid on them as the first step in the search for truth. In short, in Buddhism the Path is *trodden* rather than *discussed*. As Lakshmi Narasu points out: "No man can truly call himself a Buddhist if he has not entered the Noble Eightfold Path . . . . which represents the morality of Buddhism, and in Buddhism the moral life is no mere adjunct but its very core and essence. He who has merely understood the Dhamma, but has not shaped his life and thought in accordance with its spirit is like one who, having read a book on cookery, imagines he has eaten the food therein described." (*Essence of Buddhism*, p. 224.)

The Basis of Morality.

Q. But what is the basis or sanction of Buddhist morality?

A. At its lowest, as in all morality, purely selfish. An understanding of the law of Karma makes one realise that it "pays" to be good. At this stage of evolution there is, as Mrs. Rhys Davids points out, "no other certain sanction of goodness beyond the driving force of pain waiting on immoral living, and the pleasures rewarding moral living, now or in the long run." (*Buddhism*, p. 121.) This, when all is said and done, is the sanction of all man-made laws, and the Buddhist knows that the moral laws of nature carry with them both the punishment of disobedience and the virtuous man's reward.

Later comes the rational basis of morality in an understanding of life's unity. If life be one, each unit of that life reacts in all it does for good or evil on each other unit of the whole. Hence, to do evil, even to oneself, is to harm one's fellow men, while the strict morality of one such unit raises the level of all humanity. Finally we reach the ideal stage of "motiveless morality," a realisation that the highest virtue is in truth its own reward. "Virtue rewards itself," says Edmond Holmes, "by strengthening the will, by subduing unworthy desire, by generating knowledge of reality, by giving inward peace. Sin punishes itself by weakening the will, by inflaming unworthy desire, by generating delusions, by breeding fever and unrest. For sin to be "forgiven" is as impossible as for virtue to forego its reward. To walk in the Path is its own reward, for the Path is lit by the ever-deepening foreglow of its goal. To depart from the Path is its own punishment, for the erring steps must, *at whatever cost*, be retraced." (*Creed of Buddha*, p. 94.)

It is said in the *Digha Nikaya* that the motives of wrongdoing are always one of four: desire, hatred, delusion, or fear, and the practice of the Eightfold Path removes the power of these deadly four. Henceforth the Pilgrim lives the loftiest of ethics every hour of the day because he knows that such and only such is perfectly in harmony with the law by which he lives. Hence the advice to

"Live by law,
Acting the law we live by without fear,
(For) because right is right, to follow right
Were wisdom, in the scorn of consequence."
(From Tennyson's "*Oenone*.")

Such is indeed the voice of wisdom, even as Shakespeare pointed out when he makes Polonius in *Hamlet* say:

"This above all. To thine own self be true,
And it must follow, as the night the day,
Thou canst not then be false to any man."

Hence is the Path both simple and profound, simple in the clarity of its principles, profound in that its precepts rest on no external force, of God or man, but on the bedrock of immutable and natural law. It follows that the breach of any one of them is ultimately punished as unerringly as disobedience to the laws of health. There is here no question of the "will of God." The Path knows no authority save the Universal Law of which it is the manifested code, and the All-Enlightened One who taught it to mankind could only draw attention to its presence in each human heart, for "Buddhas do but point the Way."

But no man ever turned to ethics as the way out from life's suffering until he had realised the Signs of Being and the Noble Truths, and knowing life for what it is, set out to find at any cost some means of liberation from its Wheel.

Q. What then is the Eightfold Path?

A. We quote from the fourth of a series of articles on Buddhism contributed by the Buddhist Lodge to the *Theosophical Review*. This article on "The Noble Eightfold Path" appeared in April, 1926. It is a system of self-development according to law, a graded process of moral evolution within the law of Karma. It is the Middle Way between the two extremes of unnatural asceticism and self-indulgence. No two scholars have ever translated the eight terms by the same English words, for each term represents a concept only to be fully understood by the "ever open eye" of *Buddhi* (the faculty of intuition or spiritual perception). Meanwhile we give our own translation as at least affording a coherent, graduated code of ethics, each step following on the one before, yet each a complete and necessary precept in itself.

The Eightfold Path consists of Right Understanding, Right Views or Motives, Right Speech, Right Action, Right Means of Livelihood, Right Effort, Right Recollectedness, and Right Meditation. The word Right is equivalent to the Latin Summum or highest, best, and means that quality in its highest or most perfect form. The steps are to be taken together, though their perfection will only be attained *seriatim*, as will presently appear. Each wayfarer must tread this High Road for himself, realising that the moral and the mental worlds are ruled by laws as rigid and reliable as those discovered by the Science of the West. Truly the Buddhist "lives by law, acting the Law he lives by without fear." Hence his scorn of ritual and priests; of Intercessors and "forgiveness of sins." Knowing full well he is the child of Karma and the nurseling of unswerving law he is content to "work out his own salvation with diligence." Hence that dignity of self-reliance that marks the humblest Pilgrim of the Middle Way.

We will now consider the steps in turn.

1. *Samma Ditthi* or Right Understanding, means an intellectual grasp of the Teaching of the Dhamma, a realisation of the Three Signs of Being, the Noble Truths, the nature of self and the law of Karma.

2. *Samma Sankappo* or Right Attitude of Mind, covers motive, the use to which all subsequent development should be put—the helping of our fellow men. It is Right Desire, the Path of altruism and the slaying of self. Every Path, and sub-division of the Path, has two aspects, its right hand and its left, the right hand leading to the welfare of humanity, and the left through selfishness to spiritual death. The difference between the two is but the motive behind the acquisition of the powers therein obtained. 'It is he alone who has the love of humanity at heart, who is capable of grasping thoroughly the idea of a regenerating practical Brotherhood who is entitled to the possession of our secrets. He alone . . . will never misuse his powers, as

there will be no fear that he would turn them to selfish ends." (*Mahatma Letters* 252.) The combined action of these two steps having prepared the Pilgrim's mind, the third, fourth and fifth direct how such mentality should be applied; for as we think, we act, and action is precipitated thought.

3. *Samma Vacha* or Right Speech, needs little comment. Its essence is control, until our every word is courteous, considerate, and scrupulously true. All idle gossip and unprofitable talk must be stamped out. Silence should be so respected that the words which break it must be such as to leave the world the better for their birth.

4. *Samma Kammanto* or Right Action, is the keynote of the Eightfold Path, for Buddhism is a religion of action, not belief. Action is twofold; positive, or what we do; negative, or what we refrain from doing. The negative aspect is expressed in *Pancha Sila*, the Five Precepts or vows to abstain from killing, stealing, sensuality, slander and intoxicating liquors and drugs. But the Tathagata laid down in terms what the Christians have almost ignored in their interpretation of their own faith, that these precepts apply equally to the mind. Murder is none the less murder in that it never left the heart, and a slanderous thought is as harmful to its thinker and his enemies as any spoken word. Again, it is possible to get drunk on excitement; theft is no less theft because it wears the cloak of custom, and a lustful thought befouls its owner's purity.

The Five Precepts.

These five rules or Precepts, says Mr. Edmond Holmes, " indicate five arterial directions in which the Buddhist's self-control is to be exercised. Thus, the first rule calls upon him to control the passion of anger, the second, the desire for material possessions, the third, the lusts of the flesh, the fourth, cowardice and malevolence (the chief causes of untruthfulness), the fifth, the craving for unwholesome excitement." (*The Creed of Buddha*, p. 73.)

The first of the five is usually translated, " I promise to abstain from the taking of life," the promise in each case being made to oneself, not to some external being. As is said in the Buddhist Scriptures, " As I am, so are these. As these are, so am I." Thus identifying himself with others the wise man neither kills nor causes to be killed " (*Sutta Nipata*). And again, " Whoso strives only for his own happiness, and so doing hurts or kills living creatures which also seek for happiness, he shall find no happiness after death " (*Dhammapada*). And yet again: " In this sense we are our brother's keepers, that if we injure them we are responsible. Therefore our duty is, so vigilantly to control ourselves that we may injure none, and for this there is no substitute, all other duties take a lower place and are dependent on it." (From the *Sayings of Tsiang Samdup* in Talbot Mundy's " *Om.*")

This precept is to be found in almost every code of ethics, for life being one, the sanctity of life must obviously be that maxim's first corollary. Such is the principle, and each must use his common-sense in applying it to the needs of daily life. Clearly, killing for sport or for personal adornment can never be defended, but in the far more difficult problems of the extermination of vermin, of killing for food, and in self-defence, no dogmatic statements may be made. The Law is plain, that Life is sacred, be it that of a butterfly or man. Let each, then, cultivate within his heart a genuine compassion for all forms of life, based on a reverence for its source and the oneness which such source entails, and common-sense decisions will be made in every case in which decision as to its application must be made. But while the prevailing Western inconsistency upon such questions still prevails, such sweet compassion is but a dim ideal. How is it that we prosecute for cruelty to animals and for individual murder of humanity, yet actually sanctify the murder of flesh, fish and fowl by giving it the name of sport, and in the name of "self-defensive war" proceed to murder millions in a year? Not until the men of Europe see the wisdom of the Buddha's Teaching, or the voice of woman, ever instinct with compassion, is raised loudly enough to be obeyed, will such anomalies cease to stain the honour of humanity.

With regard to the killing of animals for food, it is obvious that the purer the food we eat the more fit will our bodies become for the functioning of our inner faculties, but once more common-sense must be employed. A Buddhist's first requirement is a healthy body in which to work. He must therefore eat such food as long experience has shown to be, not the most pleasing to his palate, but most suited to his health. To make oneself ill by insufficient nutriment is a form of vanity. Diet is not a matter of religion, but of climate, occupation and individual temperament. Indeed, Narasu quotes the Buddha as saying: "My disciples have permission to eat whatever food it is customary to eat in any place or country, provided it is done without indulgence of the appetite, or evil desire" (*Essence of Buddhism*, p. 74.) The same writer quotes also the philosopher I-tsing as saying: "To keep our bodies in health and our work in progress is the Buddha's sincere instruction to us; self-mortification and toil are the teaching of heretics" (*Ibid.*, 75.)

It is the *craving* for food of this or that description that really harms the man. If he can live on a meatless diet and still retain his normal strength it is clearly his duty to do so, but not to the detriment of far more important duties, such as the effort to enlighten all mankind. The slander of one human being by another is far more cruel than the foulest torture of mere flesh and blood, and a spiteful and malicious thought does far more harm to the great commonwealth of life than does a diet of mutton chops. It is the attitude of mind that matters, far more than the outward show. As Madame Blavatsky says: "If from illness or long habit a man cannot go without meat, let him eat it. It is no crime; it will only retard his progress a little; after all, the purely bodily functions are of far less importance than what a man *thinks* and *feels*, what desires he encourages in his mind, and allows to take root and grow there" (*Key to Theosophy*, pp. 261-2), and are not Christ's reported words to the Pharisees in point? "There is nothing from without a man that entering into him can defile him: but the things which come out of him, those are they that defile the man" (*Mark* vii, 15).

The Second Precept is the equivalent of the eighth of the Ten Commandments of the Hebrew God Jehovah, and runs, "I promise to abstain from dishonestly taking that which belongs to another." This covers every form of theft by whatever euphemistic term it may be known, from mental covetousness to business methods, which, though "legal," violate the moral law. The principle is based on social "give and take," for to steal is an offence against the community of which the thief is part. As Narasu points out, the Buddhist may acquire wealth honestly to any amount, but should use it to altruistic ends, and he quotes the Blessed One as saying to Anathapindika: "It is not life and wealth and power that enslave a man, but the cleaving to them. He who possesses wealth and uses it rightly will be a blessing unto his fellow beings" (*Essence of Buddhism*, p. 83).

The third of the Precepts calls for self-control in regard to the most powerful of human instincts, sex. "Buddha said: 'Of all the lusts and desires, there is none so powerful as sexual inclination'" (*Beal. Catena of Buddhist Scriptures*, p. 198).

Hence the Buddhist attitude to women: "Is she old? Regard her as your mother. Is she honourable? Regard her as your sister. Is she of small account? Regard her as your younger sister. Is she a child? Treat her reverently and with politeness. Above all consider well this truth, that you see only the external person, but if you could only see within that body, what vileness and impurity! Persevere in such reflections and your evil thoughts will disappear" (*Ibid.*, p. 199).

Such reasoning is curious to Western minds, but really shows a higher respect than the vaunted chivalry of the West. To the Buddhist the sex of the body is a matter of karmic effect, and sexual desire a carnal appetite as natural in its proper sphere as the appetite for food. Woman is to him far more than the means of gratifying sexual desire. She too is a Pilgrim, older maybe than the man. The Buddhist, therefore, ever reminds himself of the impermanence of fleshly beauty, and concentrates his attention on the beauty of the informing mind. All visual attraction is the prompting of the lower self, the craving of the unregenerate desires. Hence the meditation on the vanity of fleshly charm, comparable to the one-time custom in the West of having a human skull grinning its message of impermanence from the midst of the passing glories of the feast. Once regard woman in this light, and sex, from its morbid prominence in Europe and America to-day, drops to the level of the well-controlled expression of a natural desire. For the Bhikkhu, however, the vow is absolute. Any indulgence in sexual activity can only result in prolonging his stay in Samsara, but for the humble "man of the world" the essence of this vow is self-control, for man must be the master of his functions, not, as is so often the case, their slave. Once again it is the mental element that matters, for this Precept is primarily aimed at the control and sublimation of desire. Mere physical control with foul thoughts in the mind is greater defilement than a natural physical outlet with a wholesome clean mentality behind. For as a man thinks, so he is

The root of the great "sex problem" of the West seems to be the failure to distinguish between control and suppression. Man can harness the fiercest mountain stream, but he cannot dam the humblest rivulet without providing an outlet for its energy. So with sex, a clean, impersonal creative force, as natural as water in a river bed, as restless and tremendous as the sea. On the physical plane we call it sex, on the emotional plane it functions as artistic temperament, enthusiasm and emotional power, while in the realm of mind it is that mighty instinct to create, the great "creative urge" which is responsible for all that man has ever made, inclusive of himself. Herein lies the essence of sublimation to choose the channel through which the force shall flow. It is but a gradual withdrawing of the creative force from purely physical to emotional or mental levels by the exercise of ceaseless vigilance and self-control.

The Fourth Precept may be here translated as "I promise to abstain from lying, slander and deceit." Once more the same two principles obtain, that this applies to thought as well as word and deed, and secondly, the Buddhist precept admits of no exceptions and is rigidly applied. Western society is honeycombed with quite unnecessary yet deliberate lies, while to lie in self-defence or in the interests of another is applauded rather than despised. Yet to the Buddhist the vow is absolute. Narasu is clearly right in pointing out that " the Dhamma regards lying as one of the gravest offences that man can commit. . . . Not only does it involve an abuse of confidence, but in its essence it is cowardice, " the desire to gain an advantage or inflict an injury which we dare not effect by open means, or to avoid a punishment or loss which we have not the courage to face squarely." Calumny, flattery, perjury and hypocrisy are forms or grades of lying ' (*Essence of Buddhism*, pp. 91-92). It is one thing to give an evasive answer, quite another deliberately to lie. The first is but withholding the truth, the second breaking it, and how shall we attain enlightenment if every hour of the day we violate that Truth which we strive so fiercely to attain? The minor forms of lying, such as inaccuracy and exaggeration, are rightly reprobated as being so many steps on the downward road to the pure deliberate lie, while slander is doubly evil, for it is but lying with the motive, in however mild a form, of hate, and the suffering which is generated day by day by spiteful gossip needs no stressing here. Unless it is our bounden duty to tell another of a neighbour's failings let the maxim stand: " Hear no evil, see no evil, speak no evil." So shall the third step on the Eightfold Path—Right Speech—be rigidly applied.

" For those who have time to criticise have time to waste, and those who blazon forth the faults of others but blazon forth their own abandonment of duty. As the *Shi-king* says: ' If my friends would reverently watch over themselves, would slanderous speeches be made?'" (From *Some Modern Failings*, by Chew-Yew-Tsang, p. 18).

The fifth of the Five Precepts, aimed at intoxication by drink or drugs, is of somewhat less importance than the other four. Indeed, there are passages in the Scriptures where it is omitted, while one of the *Suttas* or Sermons gives an alternate fifth, "To spend one's stored-up wealth in worldly enjoyments" (*Dialogues*, Part 3, p. 225). However this may be, it needs no argument to prove the evils caused by excessive indulgence in alcohol and drugs, but the same considerations apply as in the eating of meat. There is this difference, however, that while a meat diet may be necessary for some people, no healthy person really needs the aid of alcohol in keeping fit. Being unnatural to the body, any excess, however small, will cause proportionate harm. In any case it is a violation of the ideal purity, and hence, though applying to the physical rather than the moral realm, is rightly added as a precept to the more important four. The principle underlying the Precepts is the necessity for perfect mental, moral and physical control, and any stimulant, whether alcohol or drug, when taken to excess, will tend to make control more difficult. Whether the drugs be taken in a powerful form or in the milder guise of coffee, tea and nicotine, the tendency will be the same. It is for each man, having understood the principle, to apply it constantly with sincerity and common-sense.

Q. But all these precepts, like most of the

Jewish Ten Commandments, are negative. Are there no positive injunctions?

A. "Cease to do evil; learn to do good; cleanse your own heart; this is the religion of the Buddhas." Before we can be and do good we must cease to be and do evil. The Five Precepts cover the first command, but they do but prepare the way for the second of the moral trinity, *Sila*, *Dana*, *Bhavana*. After *Pancha Sila*, the Five Precepts, comes *Dana*, charity, at once the "love" and the "good works" of St. Paul, a kindly helpful attitude to all that lives, essentially active, positive, dynamic. It may be described as the practice of Brotherhood in thought, word and deed. But even as *Sila* explains how to "cease to do evil," and *Dana* is the complementary doing of good, so *Bhavana* covers the injunction to "cleanse your own heart," or, in less poetic terminology, to discipline and purify the mind by its deliberate control and exercise. This will be considered with the last two steps of the Eightfold Path.

Motive in Acquiring Merit.

Q. I understand that a Buddhist's motive for "good works" is the acquiring of merit?

A. It would be more correct to say that a Buddhist *knows* that such will be the result. His *motive* will range from enlightened self-interest to that "motiveless morality" wherein the doer acts from an abstract sense of duty, doing what he does merely because he knows it to be his duty so to act. But this impersonal attitude was ever for the few. The doctrine of merit is a useful application of the Law of

Karma to the average daily round, whereby the humblest student may continue patiently to store up merit or "good karma" by his daily acts of kindliness, knowing that in a day to come his every act will bring its due reward.

Q. But which is more important, the act or the motive?

A. Undoubtedly the motive, and for many reasons. The effects of a deed are manifold, depending on many factors. An act is the outward expression of a thought, which in turn is coloured by emotion, the latter two characteristics forming motive, good or bad. The thought and act are hence inseparable. Too often the mere outward show of charity has atrophied the kindliness of heart which, from the doer's viewpoint, is the dominating cause in moulding the result. A good deed done with a wrong motive may benefit others, but will in the end be harmful to the doer's mind, for "the *mind* is the great maker of Karma, good or bad, and hence the intention of the mind at the time of doing a good action determines the incidence of the resultant merit." (*Wisdom of the Aryas*, p. 38.) Karma faithfully rewards each action on whatever plane. Hence, for example, to found a hospital for self-glorification will bring the "good karma" of the physical act, but will harm the donor mentally by the selfishness and proud conceit of which the giving was the outward sign. Conversely the humblest thought or deed which is the outcome of a genuine desire to benefit one's fellow men will bring its own most wonderful reward. "All life is One, and charity is simply the expression of that fundamental truth in acts and words and thoughts . . . True charity is, not to give, not to help others in order that we may be helped in return; but only because giving when we can, things immaterial as well as material, is itself the rendering into terms of life of that great truth of the Oneness of all that is. . . . " (*Ibid.*, p. 92).

It follows that the merit of a deed will be proportionate to the extent to which all living things are helped thereby.

5. *Samma Ajivo*, or Right Livelihood, consists in following a trade or occupation compatible with the above.

6. *Samma Vayamo*, or Right Effort, is a necessary step between the level so far reached and the heights yet to be won. Not by dreaming in the firelight are the Gates of Heaven stormed. "This declaration of strenuousness," says the Bhikkhu Silacara, "as a vital, if not *the* most vital feature in the Buddhist scheme of salvation, may come as a surprise to those who have been brought up in the opinion current in the West that Buddhism is a religion producing a state of chronic apathy. None the less there is no room in Buddhism for the idler in any shape or form, as indeed could not be otherwise in a faith which teaches men to rely for salvation upon their own individual effort, and denies them all help from any outside source except such as is to be found in the sympathy and kindly goodwill of fellow pilgrims upon the same journey. The prize is only for the striving—for none else." (*Lotus Blossoms*, pp. 36-37.)

The Efforts have been given as four. To prevent new evil entering one's mind; to remove all evil that is there; to develop such good as is in one's mind; to acquire still more unceasingly. Right Effort involves the right use of one's energies, so directing them as to secure the maximum results with the minimum expenditure of force. This involves the whole field of modern psychology, in the elimination of every "complex" and mental inhibition which would result in friction and consequent loss of power.

7. *Samma Sati*, or Right Recollection, is the beginning of the final stage. Having acquired some degree of moral and physical control, we undertake *Bhavana*, the control and evolution of the mind. So little is its need and nature understood by Westerners that the emphasis which every Eastern school of practical philosophy has laid upon it since the dawn of history may puzzle those to whom true culture is unknown. Yet even as a high standard of ethics is a pre-requisite to a grasp of pure philosophy because of the terrible power which such knowledge gives, so mind-control in its widest sense is a vital factor in the treading of the Eightfold Path. This need of being "ever mindful and self-possessed" is insisted upon throughout the Buddhist Scriptures, the fourfold introspection being directed to the body, feelings, thoughts and ideas, each being analysed by their possessor as the actions of a headstrong and impulsive servant might be supervised by a master who demanded discipline.

Q. But thought control is practised in the West?

A. Some of its principles are now to be found in Western schools of thought, but in the East the various methods are innumerable, having in common only the common end, to make the mind a plastic and obedient instrument in its master's hands. How many in the West are filled at intervals with high ideals and principles, the practice of which is speedily forgotten in the pressure of the daily round? Hence the need for constant acts of self-recollectedness and introspection until the vague ideals of yesterday become the habits of to-day. Whatever be the Western conquest over matter we are as yet the playthings of our minds. "Concentration, or Yoga, is the hindering of the modifications of the thinking principle," the overcoming of its natural tendency to diffuseness, by learning to apply it to a single point to the exclusion of all else. Thus only can we *understand* in the true sense of the term, for "the mind that has been trained so that the ordinary modifications of its action are not present, but only those which occur upon the conscious taking up of an object for contemplation, is changed into the likeness of that which is pondered upon, and enters into full comprehension of the being thereof." (From the *Yoga Aphorisms of Patanjali*. trans. W. Q. Judge, pp. 1 and 15.) The fact that this, which is the bedrock of all mind-control, is almost unknown to the West, shows how in its zeal to master matter it has all but left untouched the field of mind. In the West man *is* his mind; in the East he develops, controls and uses it. Of recent years some fragments of the Eastern Wisdom have been published in the

West, but the latter in its newly-found science of Psychology is but on the fringe of the Mind's illimitable possibilities. For truly "all that we are is the result of what we have thought; it is founded upon our thoughts, it is made up of our thoughts." (*Dhammapada* 1.) Hence the necessity for learning the art of concentration and control of thought before we approach the final stage.

8. *Samma Samadhi*, in its lower stages, may be called Right Meditation, while its highest is the threshold of Nirvana. Once entered on this highest aspect of the Eightfold Path, and only time can separate the weary but triumphant Pilgrim from his longed-for home. This Eighth step being the seventh carried to heights far beyond the understanding of the average man, any further discussion on its nature would serve no useful purpose here. It involves the attainment of that Universal Consciousness described by mystics through the ages in a thousand different ways, yet ever incommunicable to lesser minds.

It may be described as an immediate insight into the nature of the universe and all that therein is, by a means of knowledge far transcending reason. The faculty involved is that described as *Buddhi*, already known but only vaguely understood as yet in the West as intuition or direct cognition, the essential faculty of mysticism, by the use of which each unit of evolving consciousness cognises and unites itself with the All of which it is a part.

This height attained, the Pilgrim has attained the title "free," free from the Fetters of

Avidya, Ignorance; free from the snares of self; and being free, " he knows that he is free " and finds himself upon the threshold of Nirvana, the abode of Peace.

Such then are the factors in the Noble Eightfold Path. They must be practised simultaneously, although their perfection will presumably only be acquired in a gradually ascending scale.

No step can be left out, for knowledge must be acquired and used with right motives, and applied to speech, action, and the means of livelihood. Yet these are of no avail unless directed and controlled intelligently, after which the basis of true mind control will have been laid, to culminate in time in self-perfection at the feet of Truth.

The Path is called the Middle Way, for it carefully avoids both the pit-falls of extreme asceticism and the sophistry of those who claim that self-indulgence will eliminate desire. It lies between the Pairs of Opposites whose equilibrium is Peace.

The Pairs of Opposites.

Q. What do you mean by the " pairs of opposites" ?

A. The endless series of apparently opposing principles of spirit and matter, male and female, strength and weakness, pleasure and pain, good and evil, life and death, all of which are complementary aspects of a common whole. The antitheses "of cause and effect, substance and attribute, good and evil, truth and error, are due to the tendency of man to separate terms which are related. Fichte's puzzle of self and not-self, Kant's antinomies, Hume's opposition of facts and laws, can all be got over if we recognise that the opposing factors are mutually complementary elements based on one identity." (Radhakrishnan's *Philosophy of the Upanishads*, p. 55.)

Q. Do you mean that good and evil are two extremes of equal value?

A. The Buddha compared his Dhamma to a raft to be used in crossing the stormy seas of life's illusions, and referred to it as "something to leave behind, not to take with you. Thus, Brethren, understanding the figure of the raft, ye must (ultimately) leave righteous ways behind, not to speak of unrighteous ways." (*Majjhima Nikaya* 1, 134.) Such is, however, for the average man a very distant goal. There will be time enough when one is ethically perfect to appreciate that even virtue must in time be left behind. For the present and for many lives to come the cultivation of the Good, the Beautiful and the True, is an all-sufficient goal.

Q. Then what does the Buddhist understand by evil?

A. The Buddha was content to point out its greatest cause in man, selfish desire. It is the outcome of man's ignorance. Not realising the inherent unity of life, he takes the outward, separated self to be a permanent reality, and by his selfish separative acts disturbs the harmony of all. But nothing can be manifested in a finite world without its opposite. Light implies darkness, else would it not be known as light, and how could breathing be sustained unless we breathed both in and out? Even as the rythmic double action of the human heart, the heart-beat of the Universe implies duality, a Cosmic pulse, a never-ending alternation of in-breathing and out-breathing, of manifestation and rest. So Jakob Boehme realised, and Blake, in the *Marriage of Heaven and Hell*, agreed: "Attraction and repulsion, Love and Hate, are necessary to Human Existence. From these contraries spring what the religious call Good and Evil." The Hebrew prophet may also be invoked in support of the idea: "I am the Lord and there is none else. I form the Light and create Darkness: I make Peace, and create Evil: I, the Lord, do all these things." (Isaiah, 45, v. 7.)

Have not the finest qualities in man, strength of purpose, patience and discrimination, kindness and unselfishness, been gradually developed from the ceaseless interplay between these forces? Hence suffering and evil form the soul's gymnasium in which to strengthen virtue until, like a raft which has safely borne its traveller to the farther shore, it can be left behind.

Q. Then evil is necessary?

A. That we cannot say, but that it certainly exists and that its main cause lies in man's own foolishness is obvious to every thinking mind. Man's will is a natural force, to be used for good or evil at its user's choice. Hence by his very capacity for vice a man displays his capacity for virtue. The pitiable man is he who lacks the strength of will for either, for whereas the former is a strong man temporarily following the wrong, or left-hand path, the latter is a spiritual child who treads no path at all.

Hence the Buddhist's deep compassion for all suffering. While fighting evil in whatever form he knows that it is ignorance which made his brother fall, and knows that the very depth of his descent will be the measure of his spiritual strength when an understanding of the Dhamma has turned the erring footsteps from the wrong road to the right.

Q. What then is the wrong, or left-hand Path?

A. Man has a choice within the limitations of his self-made karma, and if the power of self, the call of selfishness, so blinds his spiritual eyes that he prefers the ways of darkness to the ways of light, such will be the Path which he will tread. Nature is in one sense blind to motive. He who studies her will learn her secrets, and knowledge is synonymous with power. How that power is used depends upon the individual. If for good, his gain will be proportionate; if for evil, the transgressor is deliberately pitting himself against the whole force of the Universe. For a while he will flourish in his selfishness, but ultimately, by the process of inexorable Law, the karmic pendulum will bring him recompense. Each selfish act is a barrier between its perpetrator and the Path of Wisdom and equally a step along the Path of Suffering. The two are as the poles apart, and though the time comes when each man must definitely choose which Path he will pursue, that choice is being slowly made each moment of the day.

Freewill and "Fate."

Q. Then we are free to choose? You do not believe in predestination?

A. The Buddhist fails to see any conflict between the two hypotheses. As Edmond Holmes points out in *The Creed of Buddha* (p. 87): "the opposition of freedom to law is a false antithesis—one of the fatal by-products of the dualism of ordinary thought," for karma and Freewill are two facets of the self-same spiritual truth. "Buddhism," as Ananda Coomaraswamy says, "is fatalistic in the sense that the present is always determined by the past; but the future remains free. Every action we make depends on what we have come to be at the time, but what we are coming to be at any time depends on the direction of the will. The karmic law merely asserts that this direction cannot be altered suddenly by the forgiveness of sins, but must be changed by our own efforts." (*Buddha and the Gospel of Buddha*, p. 233.) Hence every man is free within the limitations of his self-created karma, the resultant of past actions on whatever plane.

A man may stand in a room before two doors, neither being locked, and leave the room by either. His will is "free" and he may "choose." But suppose against one of the doors he should pile a mass of furniture and subsequently fall asleep. When he awakes he will find he has no choice of exit, for one door will be barred. Suppose, too, that he remembers nothing of his previous acts. Will he be justified in loudly complaining that he had no choice of exit, and blaming "fate" for forcing him to choose which course he should pursue? But let him realise that it was he who barred the second door and he will understand that every barrier which stands between him and his chosen end can be in time by him removed. Let him remove the furniture by actions the converse of which placed it there, and once more he will find his choice is "free." Thus does the doctrine of Karma and Rebirth remove the excuse so constantly put forward in the West for evil-doing, that "I could not help it, for my hands were tied."

Q. Does the treading of the Path enable one to perform miracles?

A. There is no such thing as a miracle. Not even a Buddha can transcend a natural law. He can but use his perfect knowledge of the laws of nature to perform what the average man would call "a miracle." So would wireless telephony seem a miracle to a savage; yet is it in no way supernatural.

In the higher stages of the Path, however, certain qualities or faculties as yet unknown to the average man are gradually developed. These occult powers are known in the Pali language as the *Iddhis* (Skt. *Siddhis*) and will appear when the neophyte has developed within himself such moral strength as will reduce the likelihood of his ever using them for selfish ends. All "psychic gifts," as practised and, for a consideration, "taught" by countless "Yogis," "Seers," and other charlatans throughout the world, are as far removed from genuine occult powers as brass from gold. No true Initiate may ever sell, or even make display of such a faculty, nor may he teach it save to those both morally and mentally prepared by years of strenuous self-training. Even then these powers are never used for "showing off," as the Buddha himself enjoined. "An ordained disciple must not boast of any superhuman perfection, be it celestial visions or miracles. The disciple who boasts of a superhuman perfection, be it celestial visions or miracles, is no longer a disciple of the Buddha." (Carus' *Gospel of Buddha*, p. 121.)

Q. What is the exact significance of entering the Path?

A. "Entering the Path" has two meanings. It may mean that the average man has pledged himself to carry out in daily life as best he may the principles set out in each stage of the Path as we have given them; but it may mean much more. For in every religion and country will be found men and women who, wearied of the ceaseless revolution of the earthly wheel, have dedicated their whole being to the treading of the Path to liberation. Severing all earthly ties as soon as their karma permits them so to do, they retire from the world of men to build into themselves by strenuous effort the needful qualities to eliminate each hindering vice. These are the true saints and seers, yogis, hermits, and holy men of all the ages, either living alone or banded together for mutual assistance in monasteries, convents and communities. Of such is the Buddhist Sangha formed, of which more will be said in the third part of this book. For them the Path is no mere adjunct to a worldly life, but everything, and for such resolute few it is divided into four Stages, Degrees or Initiations. All that the humble man is doing on his daily round towards carrying out the principles of the Eightfold Path is but an age-long preparation for this final stage, when, utterly alone in spirit, man is left to face the forces of his lower self, upon whose uttermost extinction will he find himself self-liberated from illusion, perfected and free.

Q. But if you have no privileged priests or God, who is it that initiates the neophyte when he is ready?

A. When he is ready for such knowledge and therefore power as is unknown to the average man, those Elder Brothers of Humanity, the Guardians of the Wisdom, known collectively as the Sangha or the Brotherhood, and individually as Masters, Rishis, Arhats, Mahatmas, Supermen, divulge to the neophyte such of the immemorial Wisdom as he has shown himself fitted to receive. There is here no question of privilege, favouritism, chance, luck or choice. When a man has proved himself ready, none can withhold from him his due reward.

The Four Paths and the Fetters.

Q. What are the Four Paths or stages?

A. They represent a successive expansion of consciousness marked by the casting off at each stage of some of the binding limitations of morality. They are:

I. The stage of *Sotapanna*: "He who has entered the stream," which will carry him in time to the Ocean of Nirvana. This marks the definite conversion "from the ways of men to the 'Pathway of the Gods.'" It is the culmination of years or maybe lives of self-preparation, in which a realisation of the basic principles of the Dhamma has finally borne fruit in the practice of the Holy life. At this stage three of the

Hindrances or Fetters, of which there are ten in all, must be removed. These Three are the Delusion of Self; Doubt regarding the truth of the Dhamma; and Belief in the Efficacy of Rites and Ceremonies. So long as these remain the Pilgrim will be unable to progress further on the Path.

(1) *The delusion of self*: "the delusive belief that the *individual* self is real and self-existent. This Fetter is rightly placed at the head of the list, for the clinging to individuality, the desire to affirm the apparent or actual self instead of looking forward into its expansion into the real or universal self, has its ethical counterpart in *egoism*, and egoism is the beginning and end of sin." (*Creed of Buddha*, p. 77.)

(2) *Doubt*:—The removal of this does not necessitate the substitution of a blind belief, but it is only commonsense that little progress can be made in the treading of a Path while the Pilgrim is uncertain of the end to which it leads. Yet as Lakshmi Narasu points out, "Buddhism does not under-estimate the value of doubt during the period of investigation." Its doubt is "of that sort whose whole aim is to conquer itself by high aspiration and incessant toil, not of the sort which. born of flippancy and ignorance, tries to perpetuate itself as an excuse for idleness and indifference." (*Essence of Buddhism*, p. 107.)

(3) *Belief in the Efficacy of Rites and Ceremonies*:—"The disciple must free himself, first from the general delusion that correct outward action will ensure a man's salvation, and then

from the particular delusion that religious rites and ceremonies have intrinsic value" to the attendant devotee. (*Creed of Buddha*, p. 77.) Much might be written on this attitude to ritual, so directly at variance with Western orthodoxy, yet is it cardinal to Eastern schools of thought. Not by outward show or priestly ritual, by labels, dogmas, prayers and creeds is Wisdom gained, but rather by sincere meditation until the outward appearance is but a mirror to the mind within.

In short, nothing will avail in substitution of *self*-liberation. Always the Buddha taught: "Buddhas do but point the way—work out your own salvation with diligence."

Buddhism is above all others a religion of individual effort, wherein no being, man or God, is allowed to stand for good or evil between a cause and its effect. "Absolution" and the "forgiveness of sins," as understood by the average Christian, are to the philosophic mind absurd, in that they strive to separate a cause from its effect and make some other person than the doer suffer the consequences of the deed.

Q. But ceremony has its uses?

A. Undoubtedly, as a means of education, as in the Mystery Plays of the Middle Ages, as symbolic homage to a Teacher, as in Buddhist lands, and, in the hands of adepts, for invoking natural forces for the helping of mankind. The last form is, however, all but unknown in Europe, and would never be performed in public. For the rest, the way in which this Fetter has ever veiled the truth from humanity is nowhere better expressed than in the following passage from the *Mahatma Letters to A. P. Sinnett.* "I will point out the greatest cause of nearly two-thirds of the evils that pursue humanity ever since that cause became a power. . . It is the sacerdotal caste, the priesthood and the churches. It is in those illusions which man looks upon as sacred that he has to search out the source of that multitude of evils which almost overwhelm mankind. Ignorance created Gods and cunning took advantage of opportunity. Look at India, Christendom and Islam, at Judaism and Fetichism. It is priestly imposture that rendered these Gods so terrible to man; it is religion that makes of him the selfish bigot, the fanatic that hates all mankind out of his own sect without rendering him any better or more moral for it. It is belief in God and gods that makes two-thirds of humanity the slaves of a handful of those who deceive them under the false pretence of saving them. Is not man ever ready to commit any kind of evil if told that his God or gods demand the crime? . . . For two thousand years India groaned under the weight of caste, . . and to-day the followers of Christ and Mahomet are cutting each others' throats in the names of and for the greater glory of their respective myths. Remember, the sum of human misery will never be diminished until that day when the better portion of humanity destroys in the name of Truth, morality and universal charity, the altars of these false gods." (*Letter X* at p. 58.) Strong words, no doubt, but who will dare deny them? It is a return to Religion that is needed in the

West to-day, not the slavish adherence to any particular creed. It may be said that many so-called Buddhists in Tibet, China and Japan make as much use of ritual as does the Roman Catholic Church, but we reply that to the extent they do so over and above the legitimate uses mentioned, they are substituting ceremony for self-culture, rites for righteousness.

II. and III. The stage of *Sakardâgâmin*, "he who will return to earth only once more." At this stage he has to wrestle with the Fetters of (4) *Sensuality*, the lower sensuous desires, and (5) *Unkindliness* in all its forms. These are only fully overcome in the third or *Anâgâmin* stage, "he who will return no more." Of these two Fetters little need be said. The "lusts of the flesh" are man's most powerful though not most subtle enemy, and must be slain to rise no more, before the Wayfarer may reach the final stage. The Fifth Fetter embraces every form of animosity. "The disciple has to subdue all the feelings of anger, resentment, envy, jealousy, hatred and the like which spring from his sense of separateness from the rest of living things, and from his subsequent reluctance to identify himself with the Universal Life." (*Creed of Buddha*. Holmes, p. 78.) To what extent this Fetter binds each one of us must, in the hour of analysis, "give us pause," yet must the very possibility of anger in its mildest form be utterly destroyed before the spiritually adolescent man can rise to Arhatship. Western civilisation is based on competition, which produces and implies antagonism. Man against man, business firm against business firm, nation against nation and race against race, such is the Western cry. Competition has its uses, but when its usefulness is past it becomes a Fetter in the path of progress, and must give way in time to wisdom's method, which is co-operation based on mutual understanding and respect.

Nor will the Western cry avail that the ill-will is but mirror to the other man's, for "hatred ceaseth not by hatred, hatred ceaseth but by love." (*Dhammapada.*)

When sensuous desire has been transmuted into higher forms of energy and every trace of ill-will is removed, the final stage is entered.

IV. On this, the Path to Arhatship, the seeker for perfection has to overcome the remaining five of the Hindrances.

(6) *Desire for (separate) life in the worlds of form (rupa).*

(7) *Desire for (separate) life in the formless worlds (arupa).*

The former relates to the world as we know it, and to those realms beyond the grave in which, though free from an earthly body, man is no less clothed in matter, though matter of a far more tenuous form. This too is life within the whirlpool of illusion, even though, compared with earth, it seems to some as Heaven. Beyond these lie the "formless worlds," on which *arupa* levels, man, though free from material form is still subject to the limitations of existence. Clearly, therefore, desire for continued existence under any conditions will be in time fulfilled, whereas the Buddhist's aim is to free himself from all existence in Samsara.

(8) The eighth of the Fetters, *Spiritual Pride*, explains a vast percentage of man's foolishness. Perfect must he be who finally excludes it in its subtlest form.

(9) *Self-Righteousness*.—Much might be written round the placing of these common weaknesses so close to man's perfection. Ought not these Fetters to have been broken long ago? "Perhaps they ought," said Edmond Holmes, but the Buddha knew that even in the last stage of the upward Path the shadow of egoism may fall on one's thought. The man who can say to himself: "'It is I who have scaled these heights; it is I who have suppressed egoism; it is I who have won deliverance,' is still the subject of delusions." (*Creed of Buddha*, p. 80.)

(10) *Avidya*, Ignorance, is the final obstacle and father of all suffering, for had we perfect knowledge we should never err. Even as *Avidya* is the first of the Twelve Nidanas (see p. 76-80) so it is the Fetter whose removal leaves a man self-liberated from Samsara, perfected and free. "It is for the sake of knowledge—real, final, absolute knowledge—that the Path has been followed. To know that the Universal Self is one's own real self—to know this truth, not as a theory, not as a conclusion, not as a poetic idea, not as a sudden revelation, but as the central fact of one's own inmost life—to know this truth (in the most intimate sense of the word *know*) by living it, by being it—is the final end of all spiritual effort. The expansion of the Self carries with it the expansion of consciousness; and when consciousness has become all-embracing, the

fetter of ignorance has been finally broken and the delusion of self is dead." (*Ibid*, p. 80.)

Such are the Four Paths and the Ten Fetters cast off on the way. But though this higher Path needs for its treading a greater freedom from earth's ties than is possible to the Western "family man," its principles are there for all to study and apply as best they may to the daily round. By such untiring preparation is the Road made easier, that Road which all, in time, must tread.

The Four Meditations.

Q. I presume there are definite practices which help the cultivation of the needful qualities?

A. There are four so-called Meditations calculated to produce that mental grandeur which is needed for the higher stages, but these four *Brahma Viharanas* are more accurately translated as the Divine States (of mind) or Sublime Moods. They represent a constant attitude of mind rather than a subject of thought, and are outward rather than inward-turning exercises. Yet before the quality of Loving-kindness, for example, can be "broadcast" through the Universe, it must be built in as a quality of the thinker's mind, for only then will it become an habitual attitude. This instinct of sharing his spiritual treasures with his fellow-men becomes instinctive to the Buddhist; hence the phrase repeated in thought or word on occasions of every kind: "May all be happy!" The tremendous power of such an attitude of mind as a solvent of all egotism, hatred and unbrotherliness must be experienced before it can be understood.

The four are usually given as Love, Compassion, Joy and Equanimity. Of *Metta*, Loving-kindness as an active force, little need be said save that in Buddhism it is "no mere matter of pretty speech . . . for strong was the conviction that 'thoughts are things,' that psychical action, emotional or intellectual, is capable of working like a force among forces. Europe may yet come round further to this Indian attitude." So wrote Mrs. Rhys Davids seven years ago, and her words were prophetic. (*Dial. of the Buddha*, Pt. 3, p. 185.) Its method of use in meditation is beautifully expressed in the *Tevijja Sutta*: "And he lets his mind pervade one quarter of the world with thoughts of Love, and so the second, and so the third, and so the fourth. And thus the whole world, above, below, around and everywhere, does he continue to pervade with heart of Love, far-reaching and beyond measure," for he who realises to the full the oneness of his life with all its other forms will find his consciousness expand proportionately, and as he understands, so will he love, until his heart-beat is the heart-beat of the Universe, his consciousness coincident with all that lives. As Maeterlinck says: "Truly those who know, still know nothing if the strength of love be not theirs, for the true sage is not he who sees, but he who seeing the farthest has the deepest love for mankind." (Quoted in *The Divine Spark* by T. L. Vaswani.) Love has, of course, as many forms as hearts that hold it, yet in the end must the personal give way to the impersonal, the selfish to the altruistic, for *Metta* is not " love aflame with all desire, but love at peace." In the *Conversion of the King* (p. 29) the Girl who pleads with the King thinks that:

" Love is a flame,
A fierce consuming fire, that burns away
The heart of self and leaves . . but happiness.
Love is the virgin mother of all pain,
And yet this sorrow is a thing of joy.
O man, with manly eyes, can you not see
That Love is everything? "

To whom the King replies that

" Love, like Truth and Joy,
Is many-faceted. I too have met
With Love, but in her eyes was Peace, the calm
And brooding stillness of a moonlit sea.
Of old was Love—then Understanding came.
Compassion was their child. . . ."

Surely it is man's most God-like faculty, in that by its power he sees Life from its inmost centre and knows it to be one.

So is *Karunâ* born. " ' As I am so are these. As these are, so am I. Thus identifying himself with others,' the Buddhist can put himself in the place of the lowest, most degraded, most hopelessly ' lost ' of his fellow human beings, for the Buddhist *understands*." (J. E. Ellam in *The Buddhist Review*, Vol. XI, p. 182.) Compassion is the basis of morality for " we feel with and for each other because we are really one with each other. In the valuation of deeds Compassion is the touchstone which divides them into good and evil. It is no local, temporary, human code . . . it is the voice of the

Cosmos heard in the ear." (From Loftus Hare's *Mysticism of East and West*, p. 83.)

The third of the four, *Muditâ*, is given by Mrs. Rhys Davids as Sympathetic Joy, even as Karunâ might be translated as Sympathetic Sorrow. (*On the Divine States*, being her translation of Chap. 9 of Buddhaghosa's *Visuddhi Magga*.)

"Just as if, on seeing some person who is dear and agreeable, he should be glad on his account, even so he suffuses all beings with such gladness (20). The salient characteristic of sympathetic joy is gladness, its essential property the opposite of envy, its manifestation the abolition of disaffection, its proximate cause the sight of the success of others (23). To one in an ecstasy of joy, contemplating the consciousness of beings who for some joyous reason are rejoicing, his heart becomes stored with and possessed by that consciousness (28). (Thus) sympathetic joy refers either to a state of joy in others, or in oneself, or just to the feeling impersonally considered" (22).

In the higher aspects of this latter point of view Joy comes as a spontaneous ecstasy of impersonal happiness, born of a fleeting glimpse of that glory, which Tennyson in Christian terminology described as "that far-off Divine event to which the whole creation moves." Or as another poet wrote:

"Thus have I felt in ecstasy of Joy
Some vast, illimitable, God-like Power,
That seemed the very flood-tide of eternity
Sweeping me on . . ."

The fourth is *Upekkhá*, Even-mindedness or Equanimity, and is the outcome of the other three. After sharing the emotions of others in every form the Buddhist returns to a calm detachment from all emotional excitement, a restoration of the mind's impersonal serenity. "The salient characteristic of Equanimity is evolving a central position towards others, its function is seeing others impartially, its manifestation is the quenching of both aversion and sycophancy, its proximate cause is seeing how each belongs to the continuity of his own karma." (*On the Divine States*, p. 23.) But every virtue has its corresponding vice, and equanimity is not to be confused with selfish indifference to the welfare of others, which is the outcome of *Avidya*, Ignorance.

The greater the complexity of surrounding circumstances the greater the need for such dispassionate calm, and the words of the Chinese Sage in the *Tao Teh King* might well be repeated to the fretful mind of the Europe of to-day. "Aim at extreme disinterestedness and maintain the utmost possible calm." As is said in the *Conversion of the King* (p. 25):

"In the heart
Of all creation dwells this Peace, and he
Whose heart is tuned to the same rhythmic beat
That ever pulses softly through the world
By night and day, will find his very soul
Pervaded with this deep, abiding peace,
Such stillness and such calm serenity
As little empty words can ne'er describe."

Wordsworth understood the meaning of *Upekkha*. "He found that when his mind was freed from 'little enmities and low desires' he could reach a condition of equilibrium which he describes as a 'wise passiveness' or a 'happy stillness of the mind.'" He believed this was produced "by a kind of relaxation of the will, a stilling of the busy intellect and desires. It is a purifying process, an emptying out of all that is worrying, self-assertive and self-seeking." By such a method he arrived at "the central peace subsisting at the heart of endless agitation." (*Mysticism in English Literature*, Caroline Spurgeon, p. 61.) It is the finding of that "inmost centre in us all where Truth abides in fulness" of which Browning speaks, where neither of the Pairs of Opposites has power to disturb one's harmony. It is the power to inhibit one's reaction to environment so that in the midst of outward clamour one may rest at peace within.

It will be seen from the foregoing description of the Four Sublime Moods that mysticism is as much a part of Buddhism as of all other presentations of the Truth.

Mysticism in Buddhism.

Q. But what do you mean by mysticism?

A. It is described in many ways for it appears in many forms. In essence it is an intuitive realisation of the Oneness of the Universe, an at-one-ment of one's inmost being with the heart of all existence, and the knowledge that the two are one.

In the Catechism the Master is made to ask the pupil:

"Lift thy head, O Lanoo; dost thou see one

or countless lights above thee, burning in the midnight sky?

"I sense one Flame, O Gurudeva; I see countless undetached sparks shining in it.

"Thou sayest well. And now look round and into thyself. That light which burns inside thee, dost thou feel it different in anywise from the light that shines in thy Brother-men?

"It is in no way different, though the prisoner is held in bondage by Karma, and though its outer garments delude the ignorant into saying 'Thy Soul and My Soul.'" (*Secret Doctrine*, I. 120.) In the words of the Buddhist Scriptures Man's consciousness functions on many planes, and in its evolution rises from the lowest to the highest. From the level of everyday affairs it rises to the plane of abstract thought, where thoughts are truly things, from which in time it merges in that super-consciousness with which we have already dealt, and a distinguishing feature of which is an inability to communicate its ecstasy to those who have not glimpsed it for themselves.

The distinction is sometimes drawn between Occultism and Mysticism, but these again are complementary aspects of the Path, and the perfect man is a blending of the two. The Occultist conquers the Universe and therefore himself by detailed knowledge of its laws and processes; the Mystic feels and knows the unity which underlies diversity and, caring for nought else, strives in intensity of heart to merge himself in that Central Consciousness whence he feels that he has strayed.

The watchword of the Mystic is at all times

Unity; that of the Occultist is Law. The Northern School of Buddhism inclines towards the former, while the Southern School stresses the reign of Law. The mainspring of the Mystic's life is Love; that of the Occultist an ever-deepening understanding of his fellow men, but the meeting of the ways is in Compassion where the two are one, for true compassion has no thought for self-advancement, only for the helping of humanity. Then we "go forth to help, not because we are prompted by duty or religion or reason, but because the cry of the weak and ignorant so wrings our heart that we cannot leave it unanswered. Cultivate love and understanding, then, and all else will follow. Energy, desire, intellect; dangerous and deadly forces in the selfish and impure, become in the pure in heart the greatest forces for good." (From Caroline Spurgeon's *Mysticism in English Literature*, p. 136, where the whole field of mysticism *turc* where the whole field of mysticism is charm- is charmingly discussed.)

Buddhism and Prayer.

Q. But surely prayer is an expression of mysticism, yet I understand Buddhists do not pray?

A. It depends on what you mean by prayer and to what or whom you pray. If it is to the "God within," it is but meditation in its highest form; if to a personal, external God it is but a misconception of Truth. Writing on this subject nearly forty years ago, H. P. Blavatsky said that as most people "are intensely selfish, and pray only for themselves, asking to be *given* their daily bread instead of working for it, and begging God not 'to lead them into temptation,' but deliver them (the memorialists only) from evil, the result is that prayer, as now understood, is doubly pernicious: (*a*) it kills in man self-reliance; and (*b*) it develops a still more ferocious selfishness and egotism; therefore we try to replace fruitless and useless prayer by meritorious and good-producing actions." (*Key to Theosophy*, p. 70.) This does but echo the traditional Teaching of the Buddha as rendered into verse by Edwin Arnold in the *Light of Asia*. (*Book the Eighth*.)

"Pray not! the Darkness will not brighten. Ask
Nought from the Silence for it cannot speak.
Vex not your mournful minds with pious pains.
Ah! Brothers, Sisters, seek
Nought from the helpless gods by gift and hymn,
Nor bribe with blood, nor feed with fruits and cakes.
Within yourselves deliverance must be sought,
Each man his prison makes."

Q. Then Buddhists do not pray to the Buddha?

A. Not those who understand their own philosophy, and even the humblest peasant in such Buddhist lands as Burma looks upon the Buddha as a Teacher, Guide and Friend rather than as a God. The respectful homage which a Buddhist pays to an image of the Buddha in a Shrine or Temple does but symbolise his reverence and gratitude to the Teacher of the Way, who, though loved and venerated as a man, is ever recognised as a symbol of the Light of Truth within. It is noteworthy that nowhere in the

Buddhist Scriptures is the word obedience found, for such an attitude to the Buddha is unknown. The man of wisdom bows the knee to nothing less than his own Divinity. "When thou prayest, thou shalt not be as the hypocrites are . . . but enter into thine inner chamber . . . and pray to thy Father which is in secret." (*Matth.* vi, 5.)

"Our Father within us 'in secret' is our seventh principle, in 'the inner chamber' of our Soul perception. 'The Kingdom of Heaven' is within us, says Jesus, not outside. Why are Christians so blind to the self-evident meaning of the words of wisdom they delight in mechanically repeating?" (*Secret Doctrine* I. 280 *note*.)

A Buddhist of the *Northern* School might well answer your question on prayer in the words of the Secret Doctrine to which the above was a note in commentary.

"The ever unknowable and incognizable Karana alone, the Causeless Cause of all causes, should have its shrine and altar on the holy and ever untrodden ground of our heart—invisible, intangible, unmentioned, save through 'the still small voice' of our spiritual consciousness. Those who worship before it ought to do so in the silence and sanctified solitude of their Souls; making their spirit the sole mediator between them and the Universal Spirit, their good actions the only priests, and their sinful intentions the only visible sacrificial victims to the Presence." Between the two views, personal and impersonal, lies a gulf which only the growth of centuries can span.

SECTION SIX.

Nirvana.

Q. What is the nature of Nirvana, the Goal of the Eightfold Path?

A. Its nature has been quite misunderstood by certain Western exponents of Buddhism, though their error was excusable as the result of Western modes of thought. Because Nirvana literally means "extinguishing" they took it to mean the annihilation of everything which goes to make up man. This is true only in a limited sense, and is by itself misleading.

Q. What then is Nirvana?

A. It is obviously impossible to describe, and any attempt to do so is a contradiction in terms. It is, of course, no place but a condition of mind and heart, or, vaguely speaking, a "state of consciousness." It follows that no one who has not reached that level can actually know its nature. Nor could one who has done so describe it to one who has not. That it must ever remain to our finite minds a paradox is shown by the well-known lines from the *Light of Asia*:

> If any teach Nirvana is to cease,
>   Say unto such they lie.
> If any teach Nirvana is to live,
>   Say unto such they err . . .

Strictly speaking all that can be usefully said about the subject was said by the Buddhist commentator Nagasena in the words "Nirvana is!", which is a terse way of pointing out that no amount of discussion with the finite mind will enable one to cognise the Infinite. So much erroneous matter has, however, been written about the subject that we feel the necessity of giving at least an impressionist description of what it is and is not. For the rest, it must be experienced to be fully known, but one may, by the use of analogy and metaphor, present a dim foreknowledge of its mystery. One such metaphor, for example, is used in the Scriptures again and again. The world is on fire, said the Buddha, burning with unsatisfied desire, and only when the triple fires of *Dosa* (anger), *Lobha* (lust), and *Moha* (illusion), are allowed to die for lack of fuel, will Nirvana be attained. Not until we utterly relinquish all desire for the world of illusion shall we know Reality, not until the lower, separative self is dead will the Universal Self be known as One. From this point of view Nirvana is a perfect self-surrender, a ceasing of *Upâdâna* or Grasping, the relinquishing of personal desire in a realisation of impersonal unity. In this sense it is Self-Realisation in its highest form, a final understanding of the life of Selfhood in the death of self. For self is an illusion based on Ignorance, *Avidyâ*, the last of the Fetters to be broken, in whose breaking lies deliverance. Nirvana is, therefore, the antithesis of Ignorance, a state in which the Knower, Knowledge and the Known are One. Man's personality, that which is usually for him "myself," is but a bundle of attributes held together by *Tanha*, the grasping personal desires. When all such selfish longing is for ever dead the bundle falls apart, the chain of causation is broken, the wheel of *Samsara* ceases to revolve, and "the dewdrop slips into the Shining Sea." As is said in the *Parinirvana Sutra*, a Scripture of the Northern, Mahayana, School, "it is only when all outward appearances are gone that there is left that one principle of life which exists independently of all external phenomena. It is the fire which burns in the eternal light when the fuel is expended and the flame is extinguished, for that fire is neither in the flame nor in the fuel, nor yet inside either of the two, but above, beneath and everywhere." (Quoted in the *Mahatma Letters*, page 455.)

From a philosophic point of view Nirvana is the cessation of becoming, a condition of eternal rest and utter changelessness, of "be-ness" rather than of "be-ing," where all *is*, as opposed to life as we know it, in which "all is a slow becoming; nothing is." It is a freedom from the thralldom of the "Pairs of Opposites," where life is liberated from the tyranny of form. It is that spiritual perfection in which the Signs of Being have no foothold, for the cause of Suffering is gone, Impermanence has ceased to be, and the separated self is dead.

Nirvana may be regarded from the viewpoint of an observer, or from the standpoint of itself, and the faculty by which the latter feat is possible is *Buddhi* or direct cognition by "at-onement" of the observer's consciousness with the object of his search. For the vast majority of men, however, the former is the only way, and such an examination may be from the positive or negative point of view. Negatively, then, Nirvana is the absolute annihilation of man's personality, the lower separative self, the bundle of ever-changing attributes which form the outward man; but positively it is the highest spiritual bliss. When a man enters Nirvana he loses his objective existence but retains his consciousness subjectively. To objective minds among the world of men this is annihilation, a becoming "nothing," but to subjective minds he is "no thing," that is, nothing which the senses can cognise, for the condition of Nirvana may be described as the absence of anything different, separate, or distinguishable from itself.

Q. But we retain our individuality?

A. Yes and no. The well-known analogy of the dewdrop and the sea is by itself misleading, for it is said that the truth is nearer to the Shining Sea being poured into the dewdrop when, "foregoing self the Universe grows I." In the *Voice of the Silence* the two versions appear in the same sentence. (p. 49.) "Thou shalt not separate thy being from Being, and the rest, but merge the Ocean in the drop, the drop within the Ocean," while a Chinese Bhikkhu has given his conception as "the dewdrop rebecomes the Shining Sea," implying that for such a one the cycle of the going forth and the return is over, and he reassumes his former undividedness. (See Gemmell's *Diamond Sutra*, p. 11 Notes.)

Whatever be the truth of this, to the mind of a mystic Nirvana is the end of separateness. "Man's soul," says Loftus Hare, may be described as "just that which differentiates him from the Absolute, and this, when the last shred of illusion is removed, sinks back into the real, not lost or annihilated, but saved from the torment of separateness which is the basis of the illusory life." (*Buddhist Religion*, p. 29.) It follows that "it is not separateness you should hope and long for," says the Buddhist, "it is union, the sense of oneness with all that now is, that ever has been, that ever can be—the sense that shall enlarge the horizon of your being to the limits of the universe, to the boundaries of space and time, that shall lift you up into a new plane far beyond, outside, all mean and miserable care for self. Give up the fool's paradise of 'This is I' and 'This is mine.' Leap forward without fear! You shall find yourself in the ambrosial waters of Nirvana." (Rhys Davids' *Buddhism*. Putnam. p. 129.)

Once more, then, we are faced with paradox, for in one sense the dewdrop merges in the sea, in another it becomes the sea, and only in the mystic's consciousness can the eye of *Buddhi* see that the two are one.

Q. This is far from the pessimistic "end of all things" often said to be the Buddhist Goal. How does it compare with the Christian Heaven?

A. The latter varies with the individual Christian from perfect bliss to the crude absurdity of angels, harps and streets of gold. But a Christian student must note that Nirvana is not a state to be entered at death, for it may be known while still in the world; on the other hand, it may perhaps not be reached for hundreds of lives to come. The life after "death" is to the Buddhist only *this* life in another form, and is equally illusion. Heavens and Hells, for a Buddhist believes in scores of each, are so many conditions of consciousness in the period between lives, in which the individual suffers or enjoys the consequences of his actions while on earth. Whether incarnate in the world of men or, as the Westerners say, "dead," he is equally bound upon the Wheel of Illusion from which *nothing* but the treading of the Path will "save" him, that is, make him free. Heaven and Hell, "life" and "death," are both existence in Samsara, and as such inseparable from change and suffering, but the Goal of the Path, Nirvana, is above all Heavens as conceived by men, being a state beyond conceptual thought, of perfect freedom and transcendent bliss.

When what is known as a good man "dies," he may "go to Heaven," but being far from perfect, or, as we should say, being still bound by the force of *Tanha*, he will sooner or later be reborn. Meanwhile, his Heaven, or *Devachan*, will be in length and quality proportionate to the spiritual value of his life on earth, and none is permanent. But to attain Nirvana something more than goodness is required. Generally speaking, the difference between Heaven and Nirvana corresponds to that between the Western saint and his Eastern brother. In the West the practice of such ethics as were proclaimed by Christ is so comparatively rare as to elevate their owner to the rank of saintliness; in the East such conduct is known to be but a necessary step towards the entering of those higher paths which lead to Wisdom and the Power and Freedom which such Wisdom brings, to culminate upon the threshold of Nirvana.

Q. This Buddhist viewpoint seems to be unique?

A. By no means. Even the word Nirvana was borrowed from the Brahmins, with whom it is the equivalent of *Moksha* or Supreme Enlightenment. It is the Sufi's *Fana-al-fana* and the highest aspect of the Taoist's *Tao*.

Q. How would you describe it in a word?

A. PEACE, for it is Peace unutterable.

Q. And that is the end?

A. So far as the human mind is concerned, for thought can reach no further. Yet beyond it lies *Parinirvana* which is the Absolute itself, "an Omnipresent, Eternal, Boundless and Immutable Principle on which all speculation is impossible, since it transcends the power of human conception and could only be dwarfed by any human expression or similitude. It is beyond the range and reach of thought. . . ." (*Secret Doctrine*, Vol. I, p. 14.)

Such, then, is Nirvana, and beyond Nirvana—Silence reigns supreme!

Q. Then he who enters Nirvana is lost to the world?

A. While still in a human body he can help his fellow-men, but when his last incarnation is finished, he will, so it is said, be faced with a solemn choice. Should he accept the prize to which through countless lives he has aspired, he will be severed from communion with his fellow-men, and thereby from the means of helping them. Such beings are referred to as *Pratyeka* or *Pacceka* Buddhas, those who gain liberation for themselves alone, but some there are whose hearts are so responsive to the voice of suffering that they can have no rest until that cry is stilled. Such are known as *Bodhisattvas*, those who have resolved to attain enlightenment for the helping of their fellow-men, but who on attaining Nirvana find that there is a purpose nobler still, the Great Renunciation of a Bliss immeasurable that mankind may be freed from suffering. Such is the Buddha-virtue of Compassion in its highest form, to seek enlightenment that, having found it, one may use it to enable all humanity to follow in the self-same Way.

Such then is the Buddhist Goal, and such the greater privilege, to win Nirvana and refuse it lest one single cry of suffering be left unanswered in that it was never heard.

SECTION SEVEN.

Schools of Buddhism.

Mahayana and Thera Vada.

Q. You spoke of two different schools of thought in Buddhism. In what way do they differ?

A. The world of Buddhism is, broadly speaking, divided into two great schools of thought, known usually to European scholars as the Northern and Southern Schools. Members of the former have called the latter the "Hinayana," or "smaller vehicle," reserving for themselves the name of "Mahayana," or "greater vehicle." The Southern School, however, prefers to be known as the Thera Vada, or "Teaching of the Elders," for reasons which will appear later. Geographically the terms "North" and "South" are only partially true, as adherents of both schools are found in all Buddhist countries, but generally speaking the North and East of Buddhist Asia profess the Mahayana, and the Southern countries, such as Siam, Burma and Ceylon, adhere to the Thera Vada point of view. Dr. McGovern, himself an Honorary Bhikkhu of a Japanese School of the Mahayana, sums up the attitude of the one to the other in these words: "While Hinayana regards Mahayana as a corruption of the original Buddhism, or at best as a false and decadent branch, Mahayana regards Hinayana not as false or contrary to true Buddhism, but simply as incomplete, or the superficial doctrine which Sakyamuni taught to those incapable of comprehending the more profound truths of Mahayana." (*Intro. to Mahayana Buddhism*, p. 123.)

The truth, we think, lies between the two extremes.

Historically, the Theravada is the original, and the Mahayana the later form of Buddhism, but the latter claims to represent, though of course in a sadly imperfect form, such of the inner teaching given by the Buddha to his Arhats as they in their turn were permitted to teach to those who had assimilated the elementary, yet fundamental principles proclaimed to the multitude, and found in the Scriptures of the Thera Vada School.

Generally speaking, the latter is of the two more "Practical, ethical, traditional, and the Mahayana more progressive, idealistic, mystical, and metaphysical." (R. C. Armstrong, *Eastern Buddhist*, vol. 4, No. 1.) The Thera Vada is more intellectual, and favours "cold philosophy." The Mahayana is more devotional, and therefore "warmer" as appealing to the heart. The former tends to be more exclusive, teaching the necessity of liberation of the individual from Samsara by one's own unaided effort, while the Mahayana teaches that salvation cannot be achieved exclusively, but only by embracing in one's efforts all that lives.

Such lines of cleavage, fundamental as they seem, are clearly psychological in character, and therefore deeper and more universal than the historical explanation would lead one to suppose. Certainly the fundamental distinction would appear to be that between the emotions and the mind, using both terms in the highest sense as alternative methods of approaching Truth. From this in time flow the other antitheses, men tending towards a more intellectual view, which involves the austere philosophy and ethics from which those of the opposite temperament recoil; women tending towards the devotional and, therefore, more emotional aspect, with all the expansive mysticism which this usually implies. This difference is well brought out in the attitude to ritual. Some form of homage to the symbol of the Teacher of the Way is all but necessary to the average human mind, but whereas in the Southern School such worship is confined to a dignified and graceful salutation to the memory of the greatest of the sons of men, the failure of the Mahayana to lay sufficient stress upon the need of self-reliance tends to degrade such ritual to a method of vicarious salvation obtainable by slavish adulation and the constant repetition of sacred formulæ, of the meaning of which most of the users have not the slightest idea. The splendid impersonality of the Southern School, when once affected by the more emotional viewpoint of the Mahayana, tends to become the worship of personalities with all that such practices imply, not the least among these being the gradual erection of a priestly hierarchy as the *necessary* intermediaries between that Universal Law which is the only God a Buddhist knows, and the fear-infested individual who has never learned to rely upon the latent strength within. Both Schools have, of course, the vices of their virtues. Thus, while the Southern School contains a purer presentation of the Truth it claims to teach, it inevitably tends, owing to the wider range of knowledge that it lacks, to materialise and thereby make absurd the apparently simple but actually highly metaphysical doctrines which the Pali Canon contains. Conversely, the Mahayana, while offering a far wider and more comprehensive presentation of the Arhat wisdom, has in the course of time not only degraded the metaphysics that its followers were unable to grasp as such, but has allowed to creep in on the heels of ignorance a host of practices that have in some places made the name of Buddhism a byword for ignorant and slavish idolatry.

If this psychological analysis be correct, it would seem that the gradual evolution of a Mahayana school of thought might well have been foretold by a contemporary of the Buddha. As appears in the Pali Canon, the Buddha again and again laid down what he considered to be the essential philosophy of everyday life, the ultimate minimum which each must understand if he would gain his freedom from Samsara, and this epitome he called the Four Noble Truths. On all other matters he gave his teaching from the negative point of view, either by entirely evading his enquirer's question, or by answering in the negative each aspect of the alternatively expressed demand. If neither of these two methods was practicable the Buddha would maintain a "noble silence." The point of such evasion was to dissuade his hearers from the futile dialectics in which they passed their time, and to make them realise that full enlightenment could only be reached by the treading of that immemorial

Path which leads in time to the feet of Truth herself. But the human mind is lazy, and rather than develop the latent faculties within, and so cognise the Truth at first-hand, humanity has ever sought to know the Infinite while bound upon the fretful Wheel of Change. Hence the human craving for a further and more satisfying revelation of the Blessed One's Enlightenment, and hence a slow development from the fundamental principles taught by the Arhats who remained on earth when the Buddha passed into Nirvana, of that comprehensive system of philosophy and metaphysics that is to be found even in the published writings of the Mahayana School. To this extent the Mahayana was an evasion of the Buddha's clear intention that men should develop themselves to a point where they could grasp the deeper truths of life in all their purity, rather than attempt to understand them through the distorting glass of an undeveloped mind. That this was sound advice is shown by the way in which some of the purely metaphysical teachings of the Northern School have been degraded and materialised out of all recognition, as witness the doctrine of "salvation by faith," which, essentially mystic and metaphysical in origin, has in some minds come to mean the senseless repetition of a simple formula which is guaranteed to lead the sinner to the highest heaven! But, as Dr. Paul Carus says: "The Mahayana is a step forward in so far as it changes a philosophy into a religion, and attempts to preach doctrines that were negatively expressed, in positive propositions." (*Gospel of Buddha*, p. xiv.)

On the other hand, as Mr. Johnston shrewdly says in "Buddhist China" at page 79, "In the Mahayana there is an obvious tendency for morality to be subordinated to faith; and Buddhism, if it becomes more of a religion—as the term is commonly understood—is apt to become less effective as a practical guide of life."

The comparative attitude to the person of the Buddha supplies another illustration of the differing outlook of the schools. The intellectual South, however much it glorifies the Buddha, still regards him as a man; the metaphysical and more mystically gifted North discerns a Universal Principle incarnate as a Teacher of Gods and men. This is an example of the proposition so well expressed by Mr. Johnston (ibid p. 114) when he says: "The Mahayana is higher and more philosophical than the former because, under the forms of religious or mystical imagery, it expresses the universal, whereas the Hinayana cannot set itself free from the domination of the historical fact. The Mahayanist would not, perhaps, admit in so many words that his form of Buddhism is unhistorical, but he would affirm, nevertheless, that it is independent of history because it transcends it." It is in this sense that the Northern School has claimed to be a Mahayana, or greater vehicle than the limited or Hinayana of the South.

Q. Yet both schools strive towards the same Nirvana?

A. Certainly, though it is said that they differ in the means adopted to that end; that those of the Theravada strive for self-perfection in Nirvana, while the Mahayanist is oblivious to his own salvation in his efforts for the welfare and enlightenment of all that lives. But wherein lies the difference? As the Bhikkhu Subhadra admirably says: "In proportion as we educate and perfect ourselves mentally and morally, we are enabled to help our fellow-men, and to be of use to them. All real culture comes from within, and every improvement of the world must begin with self-improvement. Keeping mankind in view, let everyone work at his own perfection, and let him consider that none can further his own weal at the cost of his fellow-men; that on the other hand, only *that* benefits mankind which in the highest sense has been done for oneself." (*Message of Buddhism*, p. 62.)

It is a truism to say that before we can govern others we must learn to control ourselves, and it would seem that before we can help our brothers to escape from Samsara we ourselves must needs have reached at least the first step on the Path which leads to liberation in Nirvana. The selfishness which is by some attributed to the Southern School may have arisen from misunderstanding of the Buddha's dying exhortation: "Work out your own salvation with diligence," which means, not that in working out our own salvation we are to be oblivious to that of others, but that ultimately each man must learn to develop and rely upon his own unaided strength in the search for enlightenment, rather than seek to acquire it by vicarious means.

We consider, then, that the various Schools of Buddhism are as complementary as the aspects of the human mind which they reflect. As H. P. Blavatsky wrote nearly forty years ago, "Buddhism in the present age cannot be justly judged either by one or the other of its *exoteric* popular forms. Real Buddhism can be appreciated only by blending the philosophy of the Southern Church with the metaphysics of the Northern Schools. If the one seems too iconoclastic and stern, and the other too metaphysical and transcendental, it is entirely due to the popular expression of Buddhism in both Churches, for both err by an excess of zeal and erroneous interpretations" (*Theosophical Glossary*, p. 63).

This "blending" was to some extent effected by Col. Olcott in 1891, when he secured the signatures of representatives of most of the Schools of Buddhism to his famous Fourteen Points, which were accepted as the "common denominator" of all. For the rest, each School must seek the Truth in the way most suited to the mentality of its followers, but let not either claim to represent the whole. Truth cannot be confined to any one of its myriad aspects, and the Dhamma is above the limitations of any sect or school.

Buddhism, it has been said, has neither Rome nor Canterbury; no one man speaks with the voice of authority and no one country has the monopoly of its truth. It moves quietly across the world, knowing no home but the hearts of those who choose to make it the dominating factor in their lives. It belongs to no one period or place, and has no authority with any man save such as comes from the still small "Voice of the Silence," the intuitive authority within. In brief, the light of the Dhamma shines forth wherever there are persons who strive to embody its principles in their daily lives. If it be said that those principles seem to differ in the various schools, let it be remembered that above all doctrine stands that which is common to them all, the dominating splendour of the personal example of the All-Enlightened One.

Zen Buddhism.

Q. Are these the only Schools of Buddhism?

A. By no means. Each is subdivided into many sects, which differ on points of doctrine, either of interpretation or of application, yet all work side by side in harmony. These, however, are the two main Schools of doctrine, but there is an aspect of Buddhism which, though in one way part of the Mahayana, may be said to synthesise the two. This is known as the Zen or Contemplative School, "*Zen*" being the Japanese equivalent of the Chinese *Ch'an*, which is in turn a corruption of the Indian *Jhana* or *Dhyana*, Contemplation in its highest form of spiritual ecstasy or pure Enlightenment. As a School, Zen is described as being the Chinese application of the Buddha's doctrine of Enlightenment. The metaphysical and transcendental form of Buddhism brought by Indian Pilgrims into China in the first century A.C. failed to appeal to the practical Chinese mind; hence the development of an aspect of the Buddha's Teaching suited to their temperament. Zen is, however, far more than a local School, for it represents a universal spiritual experience. The most important factor in the Buddha's life, according to Zen followers, is his Enlightenment. His doctrines, hence the written version of them called the Scriptures, are subordinate, as being but an intellectual attempt to express the inexpressible. "When we want, therefore, to grasp the spirit of Buddhism, we have to get acquainted with the signification of the experience of the founder—experience by virtue of which he is indeed the Buddha." (*Essays in Zen Buddhism*, p. 107, by D. T. Suzuki, *to whom and to whose book we are indebted for most of our account of Zen.*) It follows that neither of the two Schools can alone be taken as the essence of the Buddha's Teaching, for both are based on doctrine, neither on his Enlightenment. This secret of Enlightenment is said by followers of Zen to have been transmitted by the Buddha to one Mahakasyapa, by him to Ananda, the "beloved disciple" of Buddhism, and through him to a series of Zen Masters of whom the famous Ashvaghosha was the twelfth, Nagarjuna the fourteenth, and Bodhi-Dharma, often known as Tamo (circa 500 A.D.) the twenty-eighth and last. All these, however, are no privileged dispensers of salvation, but, like the All-Enlightened One himself. mere "pointers of the Way."

The essence of Zen is to be found in Four Propositions. (*Ibid*, p. 7.) :—

"A special transmission outside the Scriptures;
No dependence upon words and letters;
Direct pointing to the soul of man;
Seeing into one's nature."

These four faithfully applied will lead in time to Buddha-hood. Zen is thus the very essence of Buddhism stripped of its wrappings of doctrine and intellectual belief, for though a study of the Scriptures will produce an intellectual understanding of the Dhamma there comes a time when books alone will avail us nothing. "The basic idea of Zen," says Dr. McGovern, "is that all formulated doctrines, all books, all speech and even all thought are inadequate to express the full nature of absolute truth. Consequently Zen refuses to place complete credence in any one book or collection of books. It refuses to tie itself to any doctrine or creed." (*Introduction to Mahayana Buddhism*, p. 29.)

To find this Enlightenment we must develop and use a faculty which is higher than the mind. "O Sariputra, the true Law of the Tathagata cannot be reasoned, is beyond the pale of reasoning, and must be learnt from the Tathagata." (*Saddharma Pundarika*, or *the Lotus of the True Law*, p. 39.) The power of the mind is strictly limited, as Bergson pointed out to the West last century. He considered "that the intellect had been evolved for practical purposes, to deal with material things by cutting into little bits an undivided flow of movement, and looking at these little bits. This, though necessary for practical life, is utterly misleading by itself. Reality is fluidity, and we cannot dip up its substance with the intellect which deals with surfaces. Reality is movement, and movement is the one thing we are unable intellectually to realise." (From Caroline Spurgeon's *Mysticism in English Literature*, p. 153.) "The intellect," as Dr. Suzuki says, "upsets the blissful peace of ignorance, yet does not restore the former state of things by offering something else. It is not final, it waits for something higher than itself." (p. 6.) This "something higher" is the faculty of *Prajna* or *Buddhi*, "the highest spiritual power in our possession." This is another way of saying that to find Enlightenment we must look within, and such were Bodhi-Dharma's words. "If you wish to seek the Buddha you must see into your own nature, for this nature is the Buddha himself. If you have not seen into your own nature, what is the use of thinking of the Buddha, reciting the Sutras or keeping the precepts? (*Ibid*, p. 219.) Therefore is Zen described as the art of seeing into one's own being. "Man, know thyself," said the Delphic oracle, or, as the Egyptian Initiates said: "The Light is within thee. Let the Light shine." Zen is thus much more than mere philosophy. It is a spiritual experience, self-understanding in its highest form. It is a process of direct cognition of the Truth, beginning as occasional flashes of intuitive understanding and finally becoming that state of consciousness attainable at will.

To understand Buddhism we must live the Buddha-life, for only thus can we understand his Buddhahood. Zen is thus applied or practical mysticism, Enlightenment as found in, and applied to, daily life. The very discussion of a doctrine creates a gulf between the thinker and his thought. Only in the application of a principle, in its inclusion in our very being, is it truly understood. "It must be directly and personally experienced by each one of us in his inner spirit," and this in the world of men. "Salvation must be sought in the finite itself, that is to say, Nirvana is to be sought in the midst of Samsara." (*Ibid*, pp. 11-13.) In the words of a Christian hymn, "the daily round, the common task, will furnish all we need to ask" of opportunity for self-enlightenment. In its scorn of outward show, of everything which stands between the seeker and enlightenment, Zen is indeed much more than a School of doctrine, and applicable to all men at all times in history. Most of us have some time known such flashes of immediate at-one-ment with the subject of our thought, and this it is which is the life of Zen, whose body, as a school or discipline, is only the training of this faculty that it may be used at will. The Buddhist Scriptures of every school have instances of Zen, whose origin in Buddhism is said by legend to be that once the Buddha took a golden flower, held it aloft in his hand and gazed at it in silence. At length one of those present, Maha-Kasyapa, turned to him and smiled, for he had grasped its full significance. A single flower fully comprehended is an explanation of the whole.

In its scorn of doctrine it may be said that Zen differs from the Mahayana as the teachings of Christ from developed Christianity. Hence the saying that "Zen never explains, it merely indicates," that is, it says but little but it points the Way. In itself it is nothing. It exists in the end to which it leads. Hence the Zen analogy of the finger pointing at the moon. He is a fool who takes the finger for the moon. The motive power towards Enlightenment is will, and as the object of Buddhism is the enlightenment of the will rather than its negation, Zen is rightly described as the factor which makes and keeps a religion vital, in the absence of which it petrifies and dies. It is a positive, dynamic power latent in the heart of every man, whereby he may acquire Enlightenment. "The truth of Zen is the truth of life, and life means to live, to move, to act, not merely to reflect. Is it not natural, therefore, that its development should be towards living its truth instead of illustrating it with words?" For there is nothing curious or unnatural about Zen. It is the simplest and most natural process of all, a deliberate alignment of one's inner self with that movement which is life, the life-stream of the Universe, and perfect understanding of its nature gathered on the way. Stop to argue and consider, and you find that life has flowed away from you. Only the dry bones of logic, doctrines and ideas remain. At-one your life with all the Universe and therein you will find Enlightenment.

Some Metaphysical Doctrines.

Q. Give me examples of exclusively Mahayana doctrines.

A. We doubt if there is any such thing, as nearly all Mahayana doctrines are to be found, in germ at least, in the Southern School. There are several, however, which appear in a developed form only in the Mahayana, and of these we may mention three in particular, as no textbook of Buddhism would be complete without some reference to them.

The first of these is the doctrine of *Trikaya*, or Three Bodies, the *Nirmanakaya*, *Sambhogakaya* and *Dharmakaya*. These are "bodies" or "vestures" composed of matter in a finer and more ethereal form than the physical, which are developed by the all-but-perfect man as he approaches Nirvana. With regard to the first, "the Bodhisattva develops it in himself as he proceeds on the Path. Having reached the goal and refused its fruition, he remains on earth as an Adept; and when he dies, instead of going into Nirvana, he remains in this glorious body he has woven for himself, invisible to uninitiated mankind, to watch over and protect it. *Sambhogakaya* is the same, but with the additional lustre of 'three perfections,' one of which is entire obliteration of all earthly concerns. The *Dharmakaya* is that of a complete Buddha, *i.e.*, no body at all, but an ideal breath, consciousness merged in the Universal Consciousness. Once a Dharmakaya, a Buddha leaves behind every possible relation with this earth." (Footnote to p. 76 of the *Voice of the Silence.*) Therefore an Adept who wishes to continue to serve his fellow men renounces the Dharmakaya and continues as a Nirmanakaya, in which condition or state he can remain indefinitely as an active servant of mankind.

This doctrine of *Trikaya* appears, of course, in many forms. It may, for example, be viewed in a descending scale. "The Three Bodies of Buddha are (1) the *Dharmakaya*, or Essence-body; (2) its heavenly manifestation in the *Sambhogakaya*, or Body of Bliss; and (3) the emanation, or projection thereof called *Nirmanakaya*, apparent as the visible, individual Buddha on earth." (Coomaraswamy's *Buddha and Gospel of Buddha*, p. 238.) We thus have a Buddhist Trinity comparable to the Christian

Trinity, *Dharmakaya* representing the Fatherhood of God, the Norm of the manifested universe; *Sambhogakaya* the figure or concept of the Resurrected Christ, and *Nirmanakaya* as the visible Jesus, a particular manifestation or Son of the Father. The Trinities of all religions will be found to resolve into these three constituents, for they are all based on the metaphysics of that *Maha-Bodhi* or Supreme Wisdom which they feebly represent. Whether we call these aspects of the Absolute Brahman, Vishnu and Shiva, or Osiris, Isis and Horus, or Adi-Buddha, Avalokiteshvara and Manjusri, the principle is the same, for all alike are a triple reflection in manifestation of that Ultimate Reality which, being All, can have no name. In the Mahayana it is, however, referred to in metaphysical works as *Sunya*, the Void, or "Suchness." This imperceptible and unknowable basis of all things is the "Absolute" of the Secret Doctrine and, as in Indian philosophy, is the basis on which all is built. From it the Universe proceeded, to it the Universe will in time return, and all the wisdom of men is only concerning the laws and processes by which this vast "return" is brought about.

The Two Paths.

Our third peculiarly Mahayana doctrine is that of the Two Paths, which tells of the existence of an esoteric teaching behind its exoteric or popular form. The former is known as the Doctrine of the Heart, the latter as the Doctrine of the Eye, and as is said in the "Voice of the Silence," the Doctrine of the Eye is for the crowd, the Doctrine of the Heart for the elect. The latter will ultimately be learnt by all, but for the vast majority of men the lessons of the daily round have yet to be fully mastered. Even when the time comes for the study of the Heart Doctrine in one of its many written forms, it does not follow that it will be understood. "Yet if the Doctrine of the Heart is too high-winged for thee, thou of timid heart, be warned in time: remain content with the Eye Doctrine of the Law. Hope still. For if the 'Secret Path' is unattainable this 'day' (or incarnation) it is within thy reach 'to-morrow'" (or the next). (*Ibid.*, p. 34.)

Q. What is this Secret Path?

A. All enlightenment is a process of becoming, which some Mahayanists would describe as a process of self-realisation or realisation as the Self, whereby we "become what we (really) are." This process is referred to as a Path which each must tread for himself. This Path, as we have seen, may be considered as having a lower or preparatory, and a higher or advanced, aspect, corresponding with the knowledge therein obtained. As trodden by the vast majority of seekers after Truth it is the Noble Eightfold Path as generally understood. For the single-minded, resolute, fearless few it is the Four-fold Path or "Four Paths" which we described on pp. 131-8. This is the "Secret Path" which all in time must tread.

Q. Does not the Southern School recognise this "Secret Path"?

A. Certainly, for it teaches the existence of the Four Paths of which we have already spoken, but for some reason most of its adherents deny the existence of an Inner Teaching only accessible to those who have reached these higher stages of the Path. They prefer to cling to a phrase in the *Maha-Parinibbana-Sutta* which is usually translated, "The Buddha has no such thing as the closed fist of a teacher, who keeps something back." The explanation would seem to be that given by Colonel Olcott in his *Buddhist Catechism*, a book which was passed by the leaders of the Thera Vada for use in their Buddhist Schools. "The Buddha evidently meant that he taught everything freely, but equally certain is it that the real basis of the Dhamma can only be understood by him who has perfected his powers of comprehension. It is therefore incomprehensible (that is to say, in its fulness) to common, unenlightened persons" (p. 59). A wise man does not attempt to teach the Integral Calculus or Einstein's Law of Relativity to a child of ten. Why should we suppose that the All-Enlightened One differed from all other teachers of whom history holds record, who gave but elementary principles to the multitude and reserved the deeper Wisdom for the few disciples who had shown themselves to have reached a stage at which they would understand it and be trusted not to use it to improper ends?

Always there is the distinction between the "strong meat" for strong minds and the "milk for babes." Mr. Edmond Holmes puts the matter clearly. "When Buddha told Ananda that he had kept nothing back from his disciples, he was doubtless contrasting in his mind his own methods with those of the

Brahmanic teachers of his day, who sought to regulate the lives of the people down to the minutest detail of conduct, yet gave no reason for what they prescribed, and so crushed the spiritual life of India under the burden of an apparently meaningless ceremonialism. He doubtless meant that he had told his disciples everything which it was possible for him to disclose to them. More than that he did not mean: or the stories of his silence are all untrue." (*Creed of Buddha*, p. 152.) The Buddha's Teaching was a re-presentation of an immemorial Truth, a truth which underlay the Vedas and Upanishads on which the Brahmin philosophy was built, as surely as it underlies all other great religions and philosophies. But the Brahmins of his day had claimed this Truth's monopoly, and only doled out to the people such fragments as they chose to give. The Buddha in his infinite compassion for all forms of life dared to make public, for the benefit of all, more than had ever been given out before, stressing, however, the Way which leads to Truth rather than such portions of it as he thought it safe to give. As Mr. Holmes concisely says: "The spiritual thought of India, in the days when her soul was awake and active, was, at its highest level, strictly esoteric. In the teaching of Buddha we have the nearest approach to popularising it that was ever made." (*Ibid.*, p. 248.) That the Buddha taught to the multitude but a fraction of what he knew is well brought out in a story in the *Sutta Nipata* (quoted in *Some Sayings of the Buddha*, p. 308): "Once the Exalted One, taking up a handful of simsapa leaves, said to the brethren: 'What think ye, brethren? Which are more, these few leaves that I hold in my hand, or those that are in the grove above?' 'Few in number, Lord, are the leaves in the hand of the Exalted One: far more in number are those in the grove above.' 'Just so, brethren, those things which I know by my super-knowledge but have not revealed are greater than those things which I have revealed. And why have I not revealed them? Because, brethren, they do not conduce to profit, are not concerned with the holy life, do not conduce to perfect calm, to the perfect wisdom, to Nirvana. Then what have I revealed? The Four Noble Truths have I revealed, . . . because, brethren, they conduce to profit, to perfect wisdom, to Nirvana.' "

Q. You spoke of occasional conflict between the doctrines of the different Schools. What is your final authority for deciding which is Buddhism?

The Question of Authority.

A. A Buddhist recognises no authority on this or any other point save the intuition of the individual. By this power of *Buddhi* or *Prajna* alone can we transcend the limitations of reason and know the truth first hand. This intuitive conviction is, however, of slow growth, but during its development there is, for use each moment of the day, a lesser but quite sound criterion, sanctioned by the Buddha, which we in the West would call "broad-minded common sense." He expressly told his followers not to accept anything as true because another said that it was true; nor because it was a tradition handed down through the centuries; nor because there was a rumour to that effect; nor because it was to be found in the Scriptures or was one of the sayings of an ancient sage; nor because one would like to believe it or because it was a superficially attractive point of view; nor because it was the teaching of a holy man or teacher of any kind. Our sole criterion is that to be found within. If what is written or said be reasonable and in accordance with what we have already found to be true and with our own considered judgment, let it be tested in the crucible of daily life. If when so tested it seems to be conducive to our welfare and the welfare of our fellow men, let it be added to our system of philosophy as a rational belief until such time as the light of intuition turns belief into conviction, and we may truly say we *know*.

Q. Is nothing to be accepted on faith?

A. That depends on what you mean by faith. On "blind faith" certainly not, but if it be coterminous with a provisional acceptance of a reasonable belief while it is being tested by experience, it is of course an ingredient in the Buddhist character, while if it be taken as a translation of *appamada*, which is usually translated "earnestness," it is accepted as a basic principle of the holy life.

Q. But do you not even regard your own Scriptures as authoritative?

A. Certainly not. The tendency of modern research is to show that the Buddhist Scriptures, like the Christian Bible, consist of a miscellany of writings, compiled by different authors in different centuries, nor can any, or any part of these be relied upon as being the All-Enlightened One's own words.

Q. Then you do not consider every word of them as Buddhism?

A. By no means.

As an example of their unreliability, reference is sometimes made therein to the rebirth of a man in animal form and such a belief is widely held throughout the East. We consider it, however, a degraded rendering of a metaphorical or symbolic teaching found in many parts of the world. That this is so is clearly shown by Dr. Evans-Wentz in his "Tibetan Book of the Dead," which is a translation of what was until recently an untranslated work. (*Introduction*, pp. 42-58.) He there points out that the life-principle and the form through which it finds expression are interconnected lines of evolution, and that no "life-flux" can "incarnate in a body foreign to its evolved characteristics." Nature moves but slowly, whether in progress or degeneration, and though in exceptional cases a long series of lives of retrogression may banish from the human animal everything which makes it human, it is repugnant to all nature's laws that man, whose outward form is animal but who in essence is something more, should forfeit in a single life his precious heritage.

The widely scattered stories of such obviously abnormal happenings can be shown to be symbolic, and not literal, presentations of the ancient Wisdom. For example, Dr. Evans-Wentz gives extracts from the "Republic," wherein Plato tells how the Grecian heroes chose the type of body for their next rebirth; how one desired to be a lion and another a nightingale, symbolic of a desire to be renowned for strength or the gift of song respectively. "With the assistance of symbols and metaphors," he says, "Pindar, Empedocles, Pythagoras and Socrates also taught the rebirth doctrine," and, we should add, the laws which governed it. This use of symbolism is well exemplified in the famous Buddhist *Jatakas*, or Birth Stories, which purport to be told by the Buddha of his former lives wherein, as a dog or elephant or snake he performed great deeds of virtue and self-sacrifice. This immemorial way of teaching ethics through the power of story, like the parables of Christ or Æsop's Fables, can hardly be accepted by the scholarly as literal truth, though the people's error in so doing can be easily understood. All will agree that "in the human world we find the bloodthirsty tiger-man, the deceitful fox-man, the grovelling worm-man, the industrious ant-man . . . ," and while the animal virtues, such as the ant's prodigious industry, are always held to lead to better lives, is it not excusable that he who shows forth bestial vices should be thought to return to a corresponding body in a life to come? This wide belief, then, is a typical example of the way in which the language of the ancient Wisdom, Symbolism, has been taken by the people in its literal sense and in this form embodied in their Scriptures. If, however, the Buddha's advice be ever borne in mind, such errors are of no importance, for that which remains is no less valuable.

Q. But Scriptures are either true or untrue.

A. Yes and no, for Truth to us is relative. Until we are perfect, "even as Our Father in Heaven is perfect," as a Christian would say, that is, until the part is merged into the Whole, nothing can for us be absolute. Hence no statement is necessarily true for every person at every minute. As we grow, so does our knowledge of the Truth, and what is true for us to-day may to-morrow be seen as only partially true, while the truths of to-morrow are but the tentative beliefs of to-day. It follows that truth and falsehood are rarely found apart, and if one word of the Scriptures be found in error, of what "authority" is all the rest? Better by far to rely entirely on the discriminative faculty which lies within than the frail authority of any written word.

Not that the source of a statement is irrelevant, for it will materially affect the probability of its being true. The statement of a wise man is more likely to be true than that of a fool. Such teachings as are said to be the words of the All-Enlightened One will, therefore, be received with the greatest respect. Even here, however, the Buddha's advice holds good: "Be ye lamps unto yourselves. Be ye a refuge to yourselves. Look to no external refuge. Hold fast to the truth as a lamp. Hold fast as a refuge to the truth. Look not for refuge to anyone besides yourselves. Work out your own salvation with diligence." Nowhere does he say: "Have faith in me and I will save you."

His method was to point out certain facts which all could prove for themselves and then draw simple inferences therefrom. Having found by experience that his previous teaching was true his followers naturally accepted any further teaching as so likely to be true as to be worth provisional adoption and experiment. In such a way they step by step absorbed the teaching as a tested system of philosophy whose value and validity depended on no other authority than reason in its highest form, and practical experience. Salvation by the blind acceptance of a creed or dogma is to the Buddhist mind unknown. Even in those Mahayana sects in which salvation is attained by calling on the name of Buddha it is, at least in the minds of its enlightened advocates, a symbolic invocation to the faculty of *Buddhi* or Enlightenment, which is the "God within." In brief, a Buddhist recognises no authority for any statement save its inherent reasonableness and the extent to which it is ratified by the intuition.

Buddhist Tolerance.

Q. Then presumably you allow to others the same freedom in accepting or rejecting the doctrines which you lay before them?

A. Certainly. Buddhism claims to be, and history has shown it to be, the most tolerant, in principle and in practice, of all the known religions of the world, for the Buddha's followers have always appealed "not to the sword, but to intellectual and moral suasion. We have not a single instance, throughout its history of more than two thousand years, of even one of those religious persecutions which loom so largely in the history of the Christian Church. Peacefully the (Buddha's) Reformation began, and in peace, so far as its own action is concerned, the Buddhist Church has continued till to-day" (*Buddhism*, Putnam, Rhys Davids, p. 116). Such has ever been the policy of Buddhist missionary pilgrims and such was the policy of the great Buddhist Emperor Asoka who, in his efforts to spread the Dhamma throughout Asia, widely decreed, in graven monuments which can be seen to-day, the following command: "No decrying of other sects nor depreciating of others without cause, but on the contrary, a rendering of honour to other sects for whatever in them is worthy of honour. By so doing both one's own sect and all others will be benefited; by acting otherwise one's own sect will be destroyed in the injuring of others." The reason for this is obvious. A Buddhist seeks enlightenment for himself and all that lives, and in so doing claims the right to choose what path he shall follow to that end. Recognising an equal right to spiritual freedom in all other forms of the universal life he naturally grants to them that which he claims for himself. He knows the futility of trying to convince another against his will, for none can truly enlighten another, even at his own request. At the best he can but point the way to self-enlightenment. This attitude of mind extends to differences of outlook within the Buddhist world as much as to the doctrines of other religions, which is in a way a deeper test of tolerance. Tolerance has been defined as "an eager and a glad acceptance of the way along which others seek the Truth." To apply this to the utterly different outlook of another religion is one thing. To accept as eagerly, as being just as likely to be true, a widely differing interpretation of the Dhamma itself bespeaks a greater tolerance still. Yet there are Buddhist monasteries in the East in which exponents of widely divergent points of view on Buddhist doctrine and its application dwell together in perfect harmony. This is made possible by the fact that a Buddhist monk, on entering the Order, only binds himself to obey the regulations of his monastery; his mind is always free. As Mr. Johnston says in "Buddhist China" (p. 308): "He binds himself to no Articles and no formulated Creed, and he is perfectly at liberty to use his own judgment in interpreting the sacred books and traditional doctrines of his school." In the absence of any orthodoxy or "authority" it never occurs to any Buddhist to persecute his neighbour for holding a different point of view.

Q. Yet surely Buddhists seek to convert all other men to their own beliefs?

A. You will find that they do nothing of the kind. A Buddhist regards the Dhamma as an expression of Truth, therefore as a message of universal application. Striving as he does for the welfare by enlightenment of his fellow men, he considers it his duty to place before them such of the Dhamma as he has tested and found to be true, and thinks to be suited to each individual's requirements and mentality. In so doing he has done all which it is his duty and all which he has any right to do, for each man's spiritual progress is no one's business but his own, and any attempt to make him change his point of view is regarded in the East as sheer impertinence. Where a man seems dissatisfied with his hitherto accepted doctrines and beliefs a Buddhist seeks by simple reasoning to make him understand the Dhamma, and the solution it affords to the problems which are worrying him. If the offer is refused his duty is for the moment ended, and he returns to the strenuous task of self-enlightenment.

Q. Yet Buddhism is classified as a proselytising religion?

A. Whatever a man believes to be true he will naturally wish to share with his fellow men, but a Buddhist would never have the impertinence to *force* his views on anyone. That it is his duty to spread, in the sense of making known, the existence of the Dhamma is clear from the specific injunctions of the Buddha to his followers: "Go ye, O Bhikkhus, and wander forth for the gain of many, for the welfare of the many, in compassion for the world. Proclaim, O Bhikkhus, the Doctrine glorious, preach ye a life of holiness, perfect and pure." (From the *Mahavagga* of the *Vinaya Pitaka*.) And again, in the *Voice of the Silence* it is said: "Point out the Way—however dimly and lost among the host—as does the evening star to those who tread their path in darkness. Give light and comfort to the toiling pilgrim and seek out him who knows still less than thou, who in his wretched desolation sits starving for the bread of Wisdom—let him hear the Law" (p. 37). To teach but never to compel; to be ready to assist without attempting to convert, such is the Buddhist ideal.

Q. Then you welcome Christian missionaries in Buddhist countries?

A. If in all sincerity they consider, having studied Buddhism, that their own religion has proved, and would prove in the East, more practical in helping men towards enlightenment, by all means let them preach the Message of their Master, as they understand it, where they will. Such a qualified mission in the name of Jesus is, however, all too rare, for the average missionary's intolerance and ignorance betrays him from the first. Is it surprising, then, that the immemorial East, with its heritage of spiritual wisdom, regards as gross impertinence the efforts of the youthful West to save them from a fate in which no thinking man believes, by methods which no Christian nation has adopted for itself? Why is the West so anxious to export the wisdom for which it has no use at home? Our Eastern brothers, for example, know that life is one and therefore sacred. We in the West kill animals not only for food and clothing and for personal adornment, but even for the sake of killing, so that it be honoured with the name of sport, and who but Christians would torture animals in the utterly mistaken belief that by such means they are entitled to discover knowledge useful to humanity? Yet these are they who preach to the East of love to all that lives!

It is said that life in the East is lightly held, but what is the murder of an individual by his ignorant and foolish brother compared to the wholesale murders, committed in the name of God by nations claiming to be civilised, which, in the name of War, befouls the pages of our Western history? Again, Brahmins, Buddhists and Mahommedans abstain from alcohol as part of their accepted code of life, and it is only Western influence which has made so many of them faithless to their principles. Yet Westerners, whose cities flaunt a public-house at every turn, go forth to preach to them of abstinence and self-control!

Most Christian missionaries seem to think their Message is a new one, yet all which they *believe*, the Sages of the East had either proved or disproved centuries before the "Prince of Peace" was born in Galilee, and have moreover, to an extent unknown in the West, applied to daily life such principles as proved acceptable. It follows that where missionaries preach, and practise, the ethics of the Sermon on the Mount they will be well received. To the extent, however, that they try to spread the dogmas of a Church which has forgotten Christ they will be quietly ignored, for in the East religion is, to all but the most degraded, a matter of experience and reasoning, and not of blind, and unapplied, belief.

Q. Then you deny the teachings, as apart from the ethics, of Christianity?

A. What *are* the teachings of Christianity? Does any Christian know? If by Christianity be meant such doctrines as vicarious atonement, confession and absolution of sins, a Divine incarnation unique in history, the existence of an everlasting Heaven or Hell to follow on a single life on earth, an apostolic succession of representatives of "God" on earth, and the creation at birth of a new and original soul, utterly distinct from every other soul, created by a personal Creator and placed at birth in a palace or a slum as it pleased His arbitrary Will, we say not only that such doctrines are, as popularly taught, untrue, but that any reasonable man can prove for himself their foolishness.

But if by Christianity be meant the personal example of the man, a life which was the embodiment of what he taught, we answer that this Jesus is accepted by many Buddhists as a Bodhisattva, one who through innumerable lives has worked towards the liberation and perfection of his fellow men. To follow such an one, in the sense of striving to live a life of equal purity, compassion and goodwill, is only following the Buddha in another name, for in the end the process of enlightenment consists in finding and developing that Buddha—or Christ—principle within, which is the faculty of self-enlightenment. It has been said that no religious teacher founds a religion or formulates a creed. He only reiterates forgotten principles and points a Way. It is the foolish zeal of those who follow him which slowly turns a guide to conduct into a rigid body of doctrine, from which the life blood gradually ebbs away and leaves but a vast disintegrating corpse, while the life finds self-expression in a more fluidic form. It is because Buddhism is something which must be experienced before it can be understood that it is still so vital in the world, and it is to the credit of the few real Christians to whom religion is a spiritual experience, a treading of the Way to Selfhood in the death of self, that the Christian Church retains such life and influence as lingers on in it to-day.

SECTION EIGHT.

Conclusion.

Buddhism and Hinduism.

Q. What is the relation between Buddhism and Hinduism?

A. That depends on what you mean by "Hinduism," for this is a modern term which embraces a heterogeneous collection of many different ideas. If by the term you mean the higher aspect of the Vedanta, the flower of Indian thought, we answer that the relation is very close. The Buddha himself was born of Hindu parents and brought up, and married, as a Hindu. It was not until he had tested and rejected the endless theorising and unprofitable argument of the religious teachers of his day that his own ideas are distinguishable from his mental background. Hinduism, as we have previously explained, was seriously corrupt, and although the Ancient Wisdom or *Maha Bodhi* was possessed by a few enlightened Brahmins, the version of it which was taught to the people was a travesty. Against this selfish and unnecessary exclusiveness the Buddha, on attaining Enlightenment, at once rebelled. He realised, as every other Teacher, that some things must be kept from those unable to be trusted with the power which such knowledge brings, but he considered that there were certain general principles which should be made the property of all men as a means of helping them to find the deeper knowledge for themselves. He therefore gave his Teaching from an entirely different point of view. Indian philosophy was mainly concerned with metaphysics and the different manifestations of Reality, and tended to regard the world of everyday as scarcely worthy to be discussed. The Buddha, however, considered that for "the man in the street" a more practical philosophy was needed, and proceeded to set out, in a form which all could understand, the way to self-enlightenment. His starting point was life, life as it is and not as it ought to be, the world as we know it with its semblance of reality and not a world of perfection to be known long æons hence. His Teaching, however, nowhere denies the truth of the Vedanta philosophy, only its then distorted and degraded form and application. He was a reformer and codifier of Brahmanism, not its antagonist. We have already shown, for example, how the doctrine of Atta or Atman in its original form is perfectly consistent with the Buddha's silence on the subject, and the same applies to the nature of the Absolute. The Brahmins spoke of this as being nought which the mind could postulate, "not this, not this." The Buddha's atttitude, a "noble silence," was, if possible, more eloquent. (For further analysis see Prof. Radhakrishnan's *Indian Philosophy*, Vol. 1, pp. 360 *et sequ.* and 469 *et sequ.*, where the above view is corroborated.)

It is therefore not surprising to find that, though driven as such by Muslim persecution from its native land, the Dhamma of the All-Enlightened One lives on in the religion which he came to purify. This modification by correction is accepted without question by most Hindu scholars. For example, Mahatma Gandhi, the famous Indian reformer, speaking recently in Ceylon, declared: "It is my deliberate opinion that the essential part of the teaching of Buddha now forms an integral part of Hinduism. . . . Buddha never rejected Hinduism, but he broadened its basis and gave it a new life and a new interpretation." (Copied from a report in the *Young East*, Vol. III, No. 9.)

Buddhism and Science.

Q. To what extent is Buddhism in accord with modern Science?

A. Its relation is that of the larger to the lesser part, in that Science, in the general acceptance of the term, is only concerned with the physical Universe, while the Buddha, after analysing such existence, showed how the emotions and the mind were subject to the self-same Reign of Law. Where, however, the two circles of enquiry intersect, the tendency of modern Science is to corroborate the Buddha's Teachings, while no one of its principles has it ever yet disproved. Day by day we hear of instances of such corroboration, of which space forbids that we give details here, while doctrines such as the omnipresence of life, the impermanence of every form of matter and its resolution into terms of force, Cause and Effect as a Universal Law, and the effect of "mind" on "matter," are slowly being accepted as the mental stock-in-hand of every Scientist. Not that we consider every branch of Science, or the whole of any branch, entirely accurate in its conclusions, nor that everything described as "scientific" must be true. How can Science claim to be the touchstone of Truth, when its acknowledged leaders are not only at variance with one another, but frequently at any given moment hold opinions inconsistent with their own conclusions of a year before? Nevertheless there is in the West a growing body of knowledge about each aspect of the physical Universe which is in entire accord with Buddhist principles, for it must be realised that the oft-mentioned breach between "Science" and "Religion" is really that between Science and, not true Religion, but the dogmas of the Christian Church.

Q. Do you say, then, that the Buddha taught the principles of modern Science?

A. The principles, most certainly, leaving to those whose special study was the physical plane of Nature the rediscovery of the working of those principles and laws. The Buddha taught that the way from Suffering was to be found within, by the slaying of the lower self or separative "I-ness" and the realization of the Self which is the Universe. These laws of spiritual development, or spiritual psychology, are the higher prototypes of the physical laws of modern Science. You have heard of the maxim "As above, so below." Even as action is precipitated thought, so the physical world is but a reflection of its mental counterpart, while the laws of matter are the reflections of the laws of mind. The Buddha expounded the general principles of the latter as the basis of his teaching, while the former are the province of scientists to-day. The relation of the two being that of object and reflection, he who studies one can by analogy and inference acquire a knowledge of the other, for both are based on an analysis of their respective phenomena, and in their conclusions they naturally agree. "Science" means "knowledge," and the Buddha taught that knowledge of the Dhamma must be acquired, as "scientific" knowledge is acquired to-day, by analysis, experiment and reasoning, not by a blind belief in dogmas or an equally unreasoning "faith." In brief, the Buddhist is a spiritual and mental Scientist.

Buddhism and Women.

Q. What is the position of women in Buddhism?

A. The Buddha gave his teaching to "all who had ears to hear," and made no distinctions of sex. After due deliberation he even admitted women into the Order which he had founded, calling them *Bhikkhunis* as distinct from the male *Bhikkhus*, and he showed quite clearly that he considered them as capable of entering the Path as men. It is true that he is said to have regarded their inclusion as likely to lessen the duration of Buddhist influence in India, but the reasons for this are chiefly to be found in the peculiar social system of his day. On the other hand there are passages in the Scriptures, for example in the *Majjhima Nikaya* (trans. in *Further Dialogues of the Buddha*, Part 1, p. 345 *et sequ.*), where the Buddha announces that the Order, to be well balanced, must contain Bhikkhunis as well as Bhikkhus, and *Upasikas*, lay women, as well as *Upasakas*, lay men. The wisdom of this view is shown by the fact that the *Theri Gatha* or Psalms of the Sisters, a collection of their writings, were held in such high esteem as to be included in the Buddhist Canon, and are regarded to-day as showing a depth of spiritual understanding as profound as that of the men.

Buddhism has ever been free from the restrictions of the Christian and Hindu attitude to women. On the one hand it has never regarded her as the Devil's instrument and the cause of all man's sinfulness, as did Christianity in the Middle Ages; on the other hand it has never made her the household drudge and slave that to a large extent she still remains in India. Read, for example Fielding Hall's description of the Burmese in "*The Soul of a People*," or any account of the Ceylonese, and it will be seen that in these typical Buddhist countries a woman from her girlhood to her death is the partner, mate and equal of her menfolk and never their servant, as in Hindu and Mahommedan lands. It is interesting to note that wherever it had unrestricted power, Buddhism has raised the status of women to a level nowhere else attained. In Burma and Ceylon, for example, their position is at its best, while in such countries as China and Japan, where Buddhism is only one of several religions, its influence has had a markedly more limited effect.

Marriage has ever been, under Buddhist influence, what it is but slowly becoming in the West, a freely entered partnership. The girl neither changes her name nor wears a wedding ring. She keeps her separate property and carries on business on her own responsibility. Her children are hers to train and educate, and at all times she retains her own ideas, habits and individuality. In this respect all Buddhists understand in Tennyson's words how

"Woman is not undevelopt man,
But diverse: could we make her as the man
Sweet Love were slain: his dearest bond is this,
Not like to like but like in difference."

Buddhism and Politics.

Q. What is the attitude of Buddhism to politics?

A. Generally speaking Buddhists take no interest in matters of mere worldly Government. They realise that "mere good government cannot lead to the dying out (Nibbana) of Craving, Resentment and Infatuation, and since the Gospel of Gautama is solely concerned with the Way to that Dying Out, it is not concerned with government at all." (*Buddha and Gospel of Buddhism*, p. 181.) This lack of interest in worldly politics is founded on the fact that forms of government are only of concern to the outward physical man, for the mind is always free. For the Buddhist, as "for Confucius, the peace of the world depends on the regeneration of the inner life of the individual. The reconstruction of the world means the reconstruction of individuals." (*Philosophy of Confucius.* C. Y. Hsu, p. 37.) A Buddhist will, therefore, to the extent that he takes any part in "party politics," presumably support that section of the community which he thinks will give the individual the greatest scope for quiet self-development, but in this, as in all other matters, his choice is absolutely free. Buddhism as such has no concern with any country's government, for its field of operation, as we hope by now to have made clear, is the inner, not the outer man.

Q. But how would you interpret Buddhist principles in terms of political theories?

A. If you mean, how is the government of the Buddhist community to be classified, we answer that it has none. Buddhism is a matter of self-discipline and development, and as such has no concern with obedience to any orders unless self-imposed. On the other hand, every Buddhist is a member of some nation and as such submits himself to that country's government and laws.

Q. But if the whole world were Buddhist, what would be its form of Government?

A. Presumably, to the extent that it encourages concerted action for the benefit of social ends, it may be described as socialistic: on the other hand, to the extent that it encourages individual self-development, it is individualistic, but if it be socialistic, it is a form that strives to level up, and not down. The Buddha certainly proclaimed a spiritual equality or brotherhood, but the standard of equality was nothing less than that of the perfect man to which all living things will in the end attain. But brotherhood does not imply equality, for brothers may be of a different age. Hence the Sangha, the Order which the Buddha founded, is "ruled," to the extent that such self-governed individuals need any ruling, by the elder Brothers' suggestions being adopted by their juniors, while the voice of the eldest will be the most respected of them all. Here we have in miniature a perfect blend of monarchy and oligarchy, while the free and open vote of all the Bhikkhus on a matter of importance represents the cherished Western spirit of democracy. It must not be forgotten that all forms of worldly government may be resolved into a matter of degree and none has any spiritual value or significance. If all men were concerned with nought but self-development there would be no need for politics as generally understood, still less for the use of violent argument or force.

Buddhism and War.

Q. Then presumably all Buddhists are pacifists?

A. Each Buddhist does at all times what seems to him most in accord with Buddhist principles, and one of these is *Ahimsa*, which is, negatively, harmlessness and, positively, goodwill to all forms of life. The Buddhist is therefore a peaceful individual, incapable of active hatred for a brother man, still less for a lower form of life. If another harms him he feels but pity in return, a genuine compassion for the suffering which the hater will experience for harbouring such evil tendencies. Not that such an attitude implies or produces weakness in any form. " It is true that Buddhism paralyses the coarse, brutal energy which manifests in the mad struggle after wealth and enjoyment, for it teaches that real happiness is not to be gained through material possessions, but only through mental and moral development." (*Message of Buddhism*, p. 80.) But in fact a Buddhist leads a far more strenuous life than any soldier, for he is constantly and unremittingly at war—within himself. "Warriors, Lord, we call ourselves. In what way are we warriors?" "We wage war, O disciples; therefore are we called warriors." "Wherefore, Lord, do we wage war?" "For lofty virtue, for high endeavour, for sublime wisdom—for these do we wage war: therefore are we called warriors." (*Anguttara Nikaya*. From *Lotus Blossoms*, p. 57.) It is a curious paradox that while such a ceaseless struggle against the forces of the lower self is being waged within, the outward characteristic of the true Buddhist is his imperturbable peacefulness. For a Buddhist fights against the inward enemies of selfishness and egotism, malice, pride and mental laziness, and in the world of men against disease and penury, injustice and oppression, and vice and ugliness in all its forms. Is not such a struggle nobler and more dignified, as well as far more profitable, than wholesale murder between brother men? A Buddhist strives towards the sublimation of warlike energy into higher forms, but he realises that war is an effect whose cause must be eradicated, and that cause, as of all other suffering, he knows to be self-seeking in its countless forms, whether of one man or a nation.

Q. Is there nothing that a Buddhist hates?

A. There is no form of life however lowly, and no man however vile, that a Buddhist hates, for hatred is the child of ignorance and a Buddhist strives to understand. When the reason for another's wrongful action is completely understood the only possible reaction is a deep compassion for a fellow being so immersed in ignorance as to act in the way he does. On the other hand a Buddhist "hates," in the sense of striving to eradicate, those things which bind mankind upon the wheel of suffering, vice and evil, in whatever form. In other words he hates and fights against the evil in his own and his brothers' natures, never those who are its temporary victims. But even here the Buddhist attitude is rather to cultivate the virtue needed than to attempt to eliminate its corresponding vice, for to think on a quality only strengthens it and makes it still more difficult to slay.

Buddhism and Beauty.

Q. You have not spoken of beauty. What is its place in Buddhism?

A. It has been said that all approaches to the common Goal may be resolved into those predominantly aiming at the Good, the Beautiful, or the True, the ways of ethics, art and philosophy respectively, though all must, of course, be perfected in the perfect man. So far we have dealt exclusively with the first and third, in that the second is on the whole a matter of individual self-expression rather than a method of escape from suffering which can be laid before the world. History shows, however, that the height of Buddhist influence in any country has always marked the apotheosis of its art. The craftsmanship of China, for example, and later the architectural glories of Japan, were due to Buddhist influence, and modern archæologists are gradually uncovering in India gems of Buddhist workmanship which in their day were the glory of that continent. That the path of beauty was for some the right way to the Goal is shown by the Buddha's words recorded in the *Sutta Nipata*. (See *Some Sayings of the Buddha*, p. 206.) Once the venerable Ananda said to the Exalted One:—"The half of the holy life, Lord, is friendship with what is lovely, intimacy with what is lovely." "Say not so, Ananda, it is the whole, not the half of the holy life. Of a brother so blessed with fellowship with what is lovely we may expect that he will develop and tread the Noble Eightfold Path." The Buddhist, however, draws a sharp distinction between the pursuit of abstract beauty and its perishable forms. Too often at the sight of meretricious prettiness "the heart is at once ensnared, because it considers not the impermanency of all such appearances. The fool regarding the outward form as an excellency, how can he know the falseness of the thing, for like a silkworm enveloped in its own cocoon is he entangled in his own love of sensuous pleasure." (Chinese *Dhammapada*. Beal. p. 181.) Herein lies the solution to the apparent paradox of a Buddhist poet. Too often in the West an artist is regarded as a mere skilful reproducer of a pleasurable sensation, whether it be an ode to a flower or painting of a woman's loveliness. No genuine artist is, however, a mere mirror to the senses. Rather he strives to express his own appreciation of the undying beauty which is ever round us, and to make its presence felt to minds less sensitive than his. Once more it is the life which is pre-eminent, never its temporary outward form.

Brotherhood.

Q. What is the most important teaching of Buddhism needed by the West to-day?

A. A spirit of true Brotherhood; not the mere repetition of high-sounding platitudes or the masking of destructive competition by an outward show of friendliness, but a genuine dedication by the individual of his efforts and abilities to the commonweal, and of nations to that " Parliament of man, the federation of the world," of which Tennyson speaks in " Locksley Hall." If to this helpful and compassionate attitude to all that lives were added a corresponding respect for others' methods of attaining deliverance, we should have that unity of independent parts which is the purest form of brotherhood. It is unfortunate that such a splendid term should have been so abused of late that it has come to mean but a vague, unpractical ideal. The West has yet to appreciate that brotherhood is not an end to be achieved, but a fact to be realised. All life is one, and therefore every form of it is brother to all other forms. But while each brother seeks to behave in a brotherly way only so far as is compatible with his own selfish interests, the practice of real brotherhood will never be attained. Progress for the whole involves self-sacrifice by its component parts, and the truest benefactors of mankind and themselves are those who have given most to the community and asked for least in return. Few thinking men would doubt that in the application of this principle lies the only genuine progress of mankind, yet those who truly practise it are desperately few. For ten who preach and advocate it there is scarcely one who strives to live it day by day. Yet Buddhists firmly hold that a principle is nothing worth until applied.

Application of Principles.

Q. Is not that too sweeping a statement?

A. We think not. To accept a principle as true without applying it in action is like buying food without eating it, or taking a ticket for a required destination without getting into the train. The mind may toy with a thought, and even intellectually accept it, but until it is tested in the crucible of daily life it is not part of a man, as the muscles of his arm are part of him, only a lightly held possession, as an ornament upon the wall. The West is full of students of this philosophy and that, who gain but a superficial mental grasp of what they study and do no more. Hence they are no better for the wisdom they have read. To them the advice of Epictetus is most applicable. "If what charms you is nothing but abstract principles, sit down and turn them over quietly in your mind: but never dub yourself a philosopher, nor suffer others to call you so. Say rather (of him who does so), he is in error, for my desires, my impulses are unaltered. I give my adhesion to what I did before, nor has my mode of dealing with the things of sense undergone any change." (From the *Golden Sayings of Epictetus*. Trans. Crossley, p. 96.) But to make a newly acquired truth a part of one involves continuous effort. "You must know that it is no easy thing for a principle to become a man's own unless each day he maintain it and hear it maintained, as well as work it out in life." (*Ibid*, p. 24.) Hence it is only those who have deliberately taken their own evolution in hand who are prepared to make the necessary effort. The rest, like a herd of sheep unintelligently grazing in the fields of sense, are little better at the end of each life for the experience therein gained.

Brotherhood, then, like other Buddhist principles, is in itself an attitude to life, a recognition of a definite relationship rather than a name for an impracticable ideal. The way in which each Buddhist lives this relationship is a matter for himself alone, but from its realisation springs the harmlessness and peacefulness, the tolerance and kindly helpfulness to all that lives which characterise the true Buddhist, as also the absence in them of desire to kill or injure others, whether disguised beneath the name of sport or business rivalry, or openly displayed as in the field of war.

Buddhist Attitude to Life.

Q. How would you summarise the Buddhist attitude to life?

A. So different is it from the average Westerner's that a sufficient explanation would be beyond the scope of a volume of this size, and in the end it must be experienced to be understood. Here we can but emphasise a few points which we may not have made clear.

Of the Buddhist outlook on the Universe little need be said. The Scriptures of the Southern

School present the Buddha as maintaining on such subjects a "noble silence" on the ground that such tremendous questions, at least to those who travail in Samsara, are of no immediate importance. There are passages, however, which hint at the teaching which appears more fully in the Mahayana School. This may be summarised by saying that Samsara, the wheel of birth and death, is but the periodic manifestation, reflection, or incarnation of that Absolute Reality which is unknowable to mortal minds. Meanwhile, whatever be the truth of such transcendent matters, there is, for immediate consideration, life as we know it, and this life is regarded as a school wherein we learn the lessons only to be learnt therein. Those who understand it best are most anxious to escape from it, but even as the Buddha taught its nature to all not blinded by the glitter of its sensuous attractiveness, so he showed them, by himself re-treading it, the Path of escape, that narrow path of self-perfection which, in this name or in that, is the only Way which leads from suffering. Nor is there any "short-cut" to Nirvana, though pseudo-Saviours by the score have claimed to have discovered one. Only by mastering the lessons of Samsara can escape be gained from it. As Ashvagosha is made to say in Carus' "Amitabha":—"It is the particular in which the universal must be realised. Mere abstract goodness will become apparent only in the vicissitudes of actual life" (p. 79). Life is a College from which all in time will graduate, but whether in countless lives to come or comparatively soon is for the individual pupil to decide. Sooner or later the lessons must be learnt, so why delay this sojourn in the school? As is said in a Chinese Buddhist work, the "Fo-sho-hing-tsang-ching":—"The impermanence, painfulness and unsubstantiality of all things meet my gaze at every turn: wherefore let me use to the utmost the present hour, firm in the conviction that now is the fitting time to seek after wisdom." (From *Lotus Blossoms*, p. 52.) He who knows this life to be but a temporary resting place grieves not to learn its true nature, and is anxious to pass on. As is said in the same Scripture:—"When the wise recognise the characteristics of this world to be transience, unsubstantiality and pain, how can they any longer find joy therein?" (*Ibid*, p. 69.) Life in itself is not worth the living. That which gives it worth is the use to which it is put and the purpose to which it is dedicated, and that purpose is to guide and assist each living thing (and there is nothing dead), to the threshold of Nirvana.

Q. Then if life itself be so regarded, presumably wealth itself is still more lightly held?

A. Even as life, wealth in itself is of no value. Its worth depends on the use to which it is put. Wisely used it is a powerful instrument for helping one's fellow men, but selfishly employed it only binds its owner still more firmly to the only sphere in which it is of use, the world of sense. Once more the ideal is the mean, neither so little as to lack the necessaries of life, and to the Buddhist they are very few, nor so much as to encumber one upon life's pilgrimage. Asked, Who is the truly rich man, a Buddhist would answer with Epictetus, He who is content. It follows that a Buddhist differs from his Western brother in the nature of true charity. A Buddhist, having given personally the necessities of life, gives in addition something he regards as far more valuable, a knowledge of the Law, the outcome of the Buddha's own Enlightenment, and thereby points the Way. Wealth may provide a palliative to *earthly* sufferings, but the Dhamma leads one to the end of suffering on every plane.

Action in Inaction.

Another fundamental difference between the Buddhist and the Western point of view is that the former is essentially impersonal, the outcome of a doctrine summarised as "action in inaction," which is easier to understand than to describe. The chains which bind us to Samsara are, as we have seen, effect-producing causes, actions which necessitate for their result the presence of the doer. Hence to be freed from suffering there must be separation from such action, or *in*action in its truest form. This, however, does not mean mere laziness or inactivity, but the absence of all personal, selfish motives from each act. Perfectly selfless and impersonal action does not, like a boomerang, return to the doer for its balancing. There is, as it were, a doing of the act, independent of the person by whom it happens to be done. A Buddhist, therefore, does not renounce action but the fruits of action, and this renunciation may in itself be made a test for the selfishness of conduct. No deed of which the doer wishes for the reward is worth the doing, for it proves itself thereby to be the result of personal desire. Had the motive been in no way personal the doer would have been indifferent to reward.

Q. Give me an example.

A. Supposing a man were to help another in distress at considerable expense and inconvenience to himself, but the friend omitted to express his gratitude. Clearly it is right to help one's friends, and therefore it is one's duty so to do, indifferent to reward of any kind. If the benefactor's motives were impersonal he would not be upset by the friend's ingratitude. For such ingratitude to " hurt his feelings " would prove his motives to have included a desire for reward. Yet personal desire is, as we have seen, the cause of suffering and rebirth, until the boomerang desire has spent itself. (A very clear exposition of this doctrine is to be found in the 18th Chapter of the " Bhagavad Gita.") The effect of such " result-foregoing " action is to cause the true or inner man, describe him as you will, to stand aloof from the mask, or personality, through which he functions in the world of sense, and hence to act impersonally. If something is worth doing and it seems to someone to be his duty to see that it is done, let him do it, regarding it, however, without desire for reward but simply as " something to be done." A Buddhist is concerned with causes, never with effects. He does what he believes to be right because he believes it to be right, and having done it is no longer concerned with the result. As Madame Blavatsky says:—" The immediate work, whatever it may be, has the abstract claim of duty, and its relative importance or non-importance is not to be considered at all." (*Practical Occultism*, p. 70.) No human mind can gauge the ultimate effect or the importance of an act. One can but do what one believes to be right and leave the result law of cause and effect.

The Meaning of Duty.

The immediate result of this impersonal attitude may be described as " minding one's own business." A sincere Buddhist is so occupied with fighting the evil in himself and in the world around him that he has no time for interference in his neighbour's affairs. True, he regards it as his duty to help his neighbour when appeal is made to him for help, or on occasions which seem to afford an opportunity for doing good, but in the choice of such opportunity he carefully discriminates. The Western habit, for example, of insisting on " saving " other people's " souls " is quite unknown to him. He knows that there is danger in another's duty and finds his time is fully occupied in the performance of his own.

Q. But surely this leads to selfish indifference to others' troubles?

A. Far from it. Buddhism is most definitely

a philosophy of work in the interests of others. As is said in the *Voice of the Silence*:—"Sow kindly acts and thou shalt reap their fruition. Inaction in a deed of mercy becomes an action in a deadly sin" (p. 31). The point is that we must do things because they ought to be done and not for the reward, however pleasant we know that that will be. As Madame Blavatsky says:—"There can be no permanent rest and happiness as long as there is some work to be done and not accomplished, and the fulfilment of duties brings its own reward." (*Practical Occultism*, p. 76.)

Q. But does not this impersonal devotion to duty lead to a very cold, inhuman attitude to human suffering?

A. The greater the doctor the more impersonal his attitude to his patients, yet is he the less solicitous for their recovery or useful in effecting a cure? While the heart is torn with emotion the eye of the mind cannot see the cause and cure of the patient's suffering. On the other hand, as we have seen, a Buddhist in his daily meditation deliberately cultivates the dissemination of compassion and goodwill. Once more the path of Wisdom lies between two extremes. On the one hand we have no right to interfere in the way in which our brother regulates his life; on the other it is our duty to protect those who need protection and to help those who need help. We have no right, for example, to attempt to "save" a man's "soul" against his will, but it is our duty to prevent him being cruel to his child.

Q. Then you support such social reform movements as tend to improve the commonweal?

A. So long as they do not encroach upon the individual's right to "work out his own salvation with diligence." As we have already shown, however, the Buddhist lays stress on what may be described as spiritual education rather than physical reform. No mere perfection of physical conditions is as valuable as an understanding of the Dhamma, for the latter helps the individual to bear his karma and finally to pass beyond its sway. Again, no follower of the Buddha who has analysed existence and the cause of suffering is seriously affected by the troubles of every day. Epictetus was a Buddhist when he wrote:—"His ship is lost." "What has happened?" "His ship is lost." "His son is dead." "What has happened?" "His son is dead." "Nothing more?" "Nothing." But that any of these things are *misfortunes* to him is an addition which everyone makes of his own" (*Golden Sayings of Epictetus*, p. 81). In brief, it is our *attitude* to events which causes happiness or woe. Learn to look upon events as mere events and eliminate the personal reaction. Learn to look upon everything which happens as having rightly happened and gradually you will come to understand the Law. An aged parent dies. You grieve. For whom? For yourself, for losing something you desired? Begone such selfishness! For the parent who, after a life well filled with experience, is resting from a life of toil before returning to learn more? Why grieve? Your goods are stolen. Clearly the theft is an effect whose cause you generated in the past. Rejoice, then, that this evil debt is paid! From such an attitude is born that imperturbable content and peacefulness which marks all Buddhists to whom the Dhamma is the central principle of life.

Peace to all Beings.

PART THREE.

THE SANGHA.

We have now considered two facets of the Triple Jewel, or Buddhist Trinity, the Buddha and the Dhamma. There remains the Sangha, which, like the other two, has an inner and an outer meaning. Esoterically, it consists of all who have reached the Arhat level and remained on earth to help humanity. In the picturesque symbolism of the Mahayana School its members form a protecting wall about the Wisdom which each one of them has gained, to protect it from defilement and misuse at the hands of all self-seekers.

Exoterically, it consists of all those followers of the Buddha who have retired from the world and dedicated their lives to self-enlightenment for the more effective helping of their fellow-men. It has no resemblance to the Christian "Church," nor are its members "priests" in the Western sense of the word, though many of them, ignorant of the implications of the English term, unwisely call themselves to Westerners, "The Rev." It is true that the Bhikkhus, as members of the Order are called, live in monasteries and submit to a discipline much as did the monks in Europe in the Middle Ages, but there the analogy ends. A Bhikkhu is neither monk nor priest, but one who has withdrawn from the householder's life to devote his whole attention to the study, practice and dissemination of the Dhamma. There are no permanently binding vows. Novices may join the Order for a specified time, and every member, whether or no he has taken the Bhikkhu vows, may leave the Order at will. In some countries, such as Burma, nearly every boy on reaching manhood shaves his head and dons the yellow robe for a period, during which time he is instructed in the Scriptures and thoroughly acquainted with the practice of the holy life. All may join the Order who sincerely wish to lead the Buddha life. There is neither caste nor colour barrier, and many Europeans are living to-day in Buddhist monasteries. In the last few hundred years the organised woman's Sangha has died out, but there are thousands of Upasikas, the complement of the male Upasakas, who, while living in the world, devote themselves to self-enlightenment. These, both male and female, strive to live a higher life than those around them as an example to the rest, and may be described as lay disciples of the Buddha living in the world of men.

The organisation of the Order is mainly territorial, that is, separately constituted for each country, but a vast expanse of Middle Asia, including South Mongolia, Tibet and other nearby countries, look to the Tashi Lama of Tibet as the spiritual representative of Buddhism on earth. With this exception, however, there is no equivalent in the Sangha of the Christian "apostolic succession," nor would any Bhikkhu claim the powers which the Christian clergy earnestly believe they wield. He is no intermediary between the layman and the Buddha as a God, nor has he power to "save" or to condemn a brother man, much less to "forgive his sins," that is, to interfere with the law of cause and effect. He has no other sanctity nor privilege than that which arises from the purity and greatness of his life, and yet so long as this be truly pure his influence is as powerful as his needs are few. Possessed of nothing save the bare necessities of life, he never begs for food in vain from the nearby villages. Nor is the reason far to seek. All men who aspire to lead a clean and noble life respect and cherish those who by their daily living set them a good example, and use their advantages of greater learning and experience in helping those less fortunately circumstanced. But the discipline of the Order is twofold. On the one hand punishment is inflicted by the elder Brothers for such offences as do not warrant expulsion from the Order, but on the other hand the vigilance upon the conduct of their lives from those who provide them with their daily food is unrelaxing as it is unmerciful to all hypocrisy. So long as he proves worthy of respect, so long is a Bhikkhu revered and venerated, but the moment he proves faithless to his vows his power and influence are gone.

The effect on the Brothers of their monastic life is manifold. On the one hand they gain the cumulative moral strength and wisdom of an enormous organisation working to a common end, the death of ignorance and suffering by self-enlightenment; on the other hand they are removed as far as possible from the distracting influence and sensuous temptations of a worldly life. From another point of view, being as they are the outward aspect of the inner Sangha of Arhats or self-liberated ones, they act collectively as a mighty focal centre for the spiritual forces of the Universe.

One of the duties undertaken by the Bhikkhus is the care of Buddhist temples, but this is quite unlike the Christian curate's appointment to a definite Church. To some extent in China, and to a greater extent in Tibet and Japan, owing chiefly to the nature of the indigenous religion, forms of ceremonial have slowly been elaborated similar to Western "services," but where the Dhamma has, in this respect at least, been handed down in all its purity, for example in Burma, Siam and Ceylon, the only "service" is a recitation of the Scriptures with a commentary thereon and the taking of Pansil by all present on occasions settled by the custom of unnumbered centuries.

The taking of "Pansil," a Ceylonese contraction for Pancha Sila, the Five Precepts (see p. 110 *et sequ.*) consists in the repetition of the formula set out upon pages 222-3 (q.v.) which will be found to consist of two parts, the "Refuges" and the Precepts, five, eight or ten as the case may be (see p. 215). It is neither a hymn nor prayer, neither sacrament nor magic spell, but an act of self-recollection, and a vow to oneself to strive unceasingly to follow where the Buddha led. It is a statement of conviction that the Triple Gem, consisting of the All-Enlightened One, his Teaching, and the noble company of those who follow in the Way, together form a mighty refuge for all who seek an escape from suffering. The effect of taking it depends upon the man. The words alone are valueless, but he who, having stated his convictions, further vows to observe the spirit of such Precepts as he chooses to repeat, will reap the benefit. It cannot be too often stated that the mere repetition of the formula does not entitle one to the name of Buddhist, whereas he who lives the Buddha life has already earned that right.

There are in all ten Precepts, five of which are taken by most practising Buddhists, while a further three are taken by many laymen on certain occasions for a definite period. It is, however, considered of more value to take and seriously try to keep one single Precept than to make to oneself a host of promises with no intention of observing them. The former leads to gradual self-mastery, the latter to inevitable weakening of the will. The three additional Precepts are to abstain from taking food at unseasonable times, referring to the practice of not eating after noon; to abstain from the use of perfumes, cosmetics and self-adornment of every kind, as giving rise to vanity, and to sleep on a mat upon the ground as a means of killing out the body's desire for luxury. In addition to these a Bhikkhu keeps a final two, to abstain from music, dancing and stage plays, and from the use of gold and silver, the latter being unnecessary in a land where food is freely given and buildings set apart for those who in return expound the Dhamma and set the example of a holy life.

It should now be clear that members of the

Order are neither intermediaries nor possessed of Divine powers which can affect another's destiny, nor are they social parasites who reap where others sow. Rather are they pioneers, those who have attained such measure of self-mastery as no longer to find pleasure in the things of sense, but who have found within their hearts an echo of the sweet compassion of the All-Compassionate One, and strive in humbleness of heart to serve the world in the rôle of teacher, guide, example and unfailing friend.

Books on the Sangha.

Eastern Monachism. Spence Hardy. 42/-.
Early Buddhist Monachism. Dutt. 10/6.
Buddhism as a Religion. Hackmann.
Buddhist China. R. F. Johnston. 15/-.
Vinaya Texts. S.B.E., Vols. 13, 17 and 20.

BIBLIOGRAPHY.

of Books on Buddhism or kindred subjects from which quotation has been made herein. There is no guarantee that the books are still obtainable, and prices are only approximate.

Amitabha.—A Story of Buddhist Theology. Paul Carus. Open Court Publishing Co. 1906. 3/6.

Buddha and the Gospel of Buddhism.—Ananda Coomaraswamy, D.Sc. George Harrap. 1916. (Reprinted 1928, at 15/-.) Illustrated.

Buddhism.—T. W. Rhys Davids, Ph.D. S.P.C.K. Reprint, 1925. 4/-.

Buddhism: Its History and Literature.—(Lectures.) Putnam. New Edn. 1926. 7/6.

Buddhism.—A Study of the Buddhist Norm. Mrs. Rhys Davids. Williams and Norgate. Home University Library. 2/6.

Buddhism: And its place in the Mental Life of Mankind.—Paul Dahlke. MacMillan. 1927. 10/6.

Buddhism and Christianity.—J. Estlin Carpenter, D.D. Hodder & Stoughton. 1923. 4/6.

Buddhism in Translations.—Warren. Harvard University Press. 8th issue. 1922. 13/6.

Buddhist Catechism.—H. S. Olcott. 44th Edn. Theosophical Publishing House. 1915. 1/3.

Buddhist Religion.—W. Loftus Hare. C. W. Daniel. Paper-backed, 1/-.

Buddhist Suttas.—Trans. Rhys Davids. Sacred Books of the East, Vol. XI. Oxford Clarendon Press. 1900. 12/6.

A Catena of Buddhist Scriptures from the Chinese.—Samuel Beal, Trubner & Co. 1871. Out of print.

Compendium of Philosophy.—S. Z. Aung. Published for Pali Text Society, by Henry Frowde. 1910. Out of print.

The Conversion of the King.—Youth Lodge, London. Theosophical Publishing House. 1925. 1/-.

The Creed of Buddha.—Edmond Holmes. John Lane. The Bodley Head. Second Edn. 1919. 6/-.

The Dhammapada.—Trans. Max Müller. Sacred Books of the East, Vol. X. Oxford University Press. 1924. 12/6.

The Dialogues of the Buddha.—Trans. Prof. and Mrs. Rhys Davids. 3 Vols. Oxford University Press. 1910. At 12/6.

The Diamond Sutra, or Prajna Paramita.—W. Gemmell. Kegan Paul. 1912. Out of print.

Eastern Buddhist.—Edited by D. T. Suzuki. (A Periodical.) Eastern Buddhist Society, Tokyo, Japan.

Essays in Zen Buddhism.—D. T. Suzuki. 1st Series. Luzac & Co. 1927. 17/6.

The Essence of Buddhism.—Lakshmi Narasu. 2nd Edn. Madras. 1912. 6/6. Illustrated.

Further Dialogues of the Buddha.—2 Vols. Chalmers. Oxford University Press. 1926. At 15/-.

The Gospel of Buddha.—Paul Carus. Open Court Publishing Co. 1917. 5/-.

Indian Philosophy.—Vol. I. Chapters on Buddhism. Radhakrishnan. Allen Unwin. 1923. 21/-.

Introduction to Mahayana Buddhism.—McGovern. Kegan Paul. 1922. 7/6.

Iti Vuttaka.—Trans. J. H. Moore. Columbia University Press. 1908.

The Key to Theosophy.—H. P. Blavatsky. Theosophical Publishing Society. 2nd Edn. 1890. Out of print. (Re-issued by United Lodge of Theosophists at 9/-.)

The Light of Asia.—Sir Edwin Arnold. Kegan Paul. 1921. Pocket Edn., 2/-.

Lotus Blossoms.—The Bhikkhu Silacara. Theosophical Publishing House. 4th Edn., 1922. Paper-backed, 1/-.

(Many of our quotations from the Scriptures were copied from this book.)

Mahatma Letters to A. P. Sinnett.—Ed., A. T. Barker. T. Fisher Unwin. 1923. 1st Edn. 21/-.

The Message of Buddhism.—The Bhikkhu Subhadra. Kegan Paul. 1922. 2/6.

Mysticism of East and West.—W. Loftus Hare. Jonathan Cape. 1923. 10/6.

Om.—Talbot Mundy. Hutchinson & Co. 3rd Edn. Reprinted at 3/6.

Practical Occultism.—H. P. Blavatsky. Theosophical Publishing House. Reprinted 1923. 2/-.

Reincarnation.—E. D. Walker & Co. Rider & Co. 3rd Edn., 1919. 7/6.

Saddharma Pundarika.—(The Lotus of the Good Law.) Sacred Books of the East, Vol. XXI. Trans., Kern. Oxford University Press. 1909. 15/-.

The Secret Doctrine.—2 Vols. H. P. Blavatsky. 2nd Edn., 1888. Theosophical Publishing Co., Ltd. Out of print. (Now obtainable two vols. in one from United Lodge of Theosophists at 30/-.)

Some Sayings of the Buddha.—F. L. Woodward. Oxford University Press. 1925. 5/-.

The Soul of a People.—Fielding Hall. MacMillan. 3/6.

Sutta Nipata.—Contained in Buddhist Suttas Q.V.

The Theosophical Glossary.—H. P. Blavatsky. United Lodge of Theosophists. 1918. 9/-.

The Tibetan Book of the Dead.—W. Y. Evans Wentz. Oxford University Press. 1927. 16/-.

The Udana.—D. M. Strong. Luzac & Co. 1902.

The Voice of the Silence.—Trans., "H.P.B." Theosophical Publishing Society. 1889. Out of print. (Our quotations from correct edn. by Theo. Pub. Co., New York. 3/6.)

The Wisdom of the Aryas.—Allan Bennett. Kegan Paul. 1923. 2/6.

The Attention of Students is also drawn to the following Books:—

Ashvagosha's "Awakening of Faith in the Mahayana."—Trans. Suzuki. Open Court Publishing Co. 1900. 10/6. Out of print.

Buddhism, the Science of Life.—Cleather & Crump. China Booksellers, Ltd., Peking. 1928. 6/-.

First Fifty Discourses of Gotama the Buddha.—Collected from the Majjima Nikaya. Trans. Bhikkhu Silacara. Now obtainable 2 vols. in one. Probsthain. 15/-.

A League of Religions.—Chapter on Buddhism. Tyssul Davis. Lindsey Press. 2/6.

The Path of Light.—Trans. from a Mahayana Scripture. L. D. Barnett. Wisdom of the East Series. John Murray. 1909. 3/6 Out of print.

The Ring of Return.—(Anthology of references to Re-birth.) Eva Martin. Philip Allan & Co. 1927. 7/6.

PANSIL (in English.)

(See also pp. 214-5).

Praise be to the Blessed One, the Venerable One, Perfect in Wisdom!

I go to the Buddha for Guidance.

I go to the Teaching for Guidance.

I go to the Order for Guidance.

For the second time I go to the Buddha for Guidance.

For the second time I go to the Teaching for Guidance.

For the second time I go to the Order for Guidance.

For the third time I go to the Buddha for Guidance.

For the third time I go to the Teaching for Guidance.

For the third time I go to the Order for Guidance.

I promise to abstain from the taking of life.

I promise to abstain from taking that which is not given me.

I promise to abstain from indulgence in sensuality.

I promise to abstain from lying, slander and deceit.

I promise to abstain from intoxicating liquors and drugs.

PANSIL (in Pali.)

NAMO TASSA BHAGAVATO ARAHATO SAMMASAMBUDDHASSA!

BUDDHAN̂ SARANAN̂ GAĈĈHĀMI.

DHAMMAN̂ SARANAN̂ GAĈĈHĀMI.

SAN̂GHAN̂ SARANAN̂ GAĈĈHĀMI.

DUTIYAMPI BUDDHAN̂ SARANAN̂ GAĈĈHĀMI.

DUTIYAMPI DHAMMAN̂ SARANAN̂ GAĈĈHĀMI.

DUTIYAMPI SAN̂GHAN̂ SARANAN̂ GAĈĈHĀMI.

TATIYAMPI BUDDHAN̂ SARANAN̂ GAĈĈHĀMI.

TATIYAMPI DHAMMAN̂ SARANAN̂ GAĈĈHĀMI.

TATIYAMPI SAN̂GHAN̂ SARANAN̂ GAĈĈHĀMI.

PĀNĀTIPĀTĀ WERAMANĪ SIKKHĀPADAN̂ SAMĀDIYĀMI.

ADINNĀDĀNĀ WERAMANĪ SIKKHĀPADAN̂ SAMĀDIYĀMI.

KĀMESU MIĈĈHĀĈĀRĀ WERAMANĪ SIKKHĀPADAN̂ SAMĀDIYĀMI.

MUSĀWĀDĀ WERAMANĪ SIKKHĀPADAN̂ SAMĀDIYĀMI.

SURĀ - MERAYĀ - MAJJA - PAMĀDA - TTHĀNĀ WERAMANĪ SIKKHĀPADAN̂ SAMĀDIYĀMI.

Notes on pronunciation.

Vowels have Italian values.

ĉ = ch in church. ĉh = ch aspirated.

k = as in English. kh = k aspirated.

j = as in joy. w = English w.

s is always as s in say, never as z.

n̂ is a nasal sound, almost like ng in king, but nearer the French nasal.

INDEX.

(See also Contents and Bibliography.)
